Life by Design

Life by Design

*Mastering Energy, Money and
Leverage in 9 Simple Steps*

Sundardas D Annamalay

Library of Congress Control Number:		2017916094
ISBN:	Hardcover	978-1-5434-0457-9
	Softcover	978-1-5434-0456-2
	eBook	978-1-5434-0455-5

Print information available on the last page.

Rev. date: 07/18/2018

To order additional copies of this book, contact:
Xlibris
1-800-455-039
www.Xlibris.com.au
Orders@Xlibris.com.au
520750

CONTENTS

Words of Praise for "Life by Design"

Dr Sundardas has once again written an invaluable piece that is critical to everyone. In it, he has outlined strategies to maximize this limited resource based on who we are and how we live our life. Most importantly, he has systematised his ideas so that anyone who reads it, can use it immediately and manifest the shifts they intend to have. The strategies and ideas proposed have been articulately placed so that we can run with it without wasting time. I have read a few books on Time Management but this one stands out as a holistic and very practical system that will change your life immediately if you implement the steps. Congrats on a brilliant piece!!

Dr Granville D'Souza, DBA
CEO of EQ Asia and author of 3 books on Emotional Intelligence (Singapore)

Practical and useful steps for anyone with the goal of mastering their time for income and profit and still have time for family, friends, and hobbies. This absorbing, easy to read book also includes psychological strategies, the timely use of technology and using your body's biological rhythms to get you where you want to be. The section on roadblocks incisively got me through to the next step of time mastery.

Chuah Ai Mee, *Award Winning Author, Entrepreneur, (Singapore)*

The title of this book is misleading, yet positively so. There is no dichotomy between Life and Energy. This book is really about Mastering Life, how we can make the most of it by focusing on the few important things we need to do that will bring us the most fulfillment. True to this principle, the author has focused on nine high leverage steps to achieve the outcomes we want in our life. One tip for readers: Don't skip the introductory steps. I like the clarity and honesty of this book.

Ajith Damodaran, *Medical Doctor, (Singapore)*

"This book has been useful to me in guiding the first steps to planning my work day in a more efficient manner. Time Management is a daunting prospect to many of us, and having chunk sizes to follow makes it easier to get started. I am currently sticking to the new program for twenty-one days, to try to make it a new good habit. Once that is done, I will look for other areas of my life to apply that to. Thanks for the great tips, Dr Sundardas!"

Lorraine Lee, *Lawyer (Singapore)*

Dr Sundardas' new book focuses on an issue seen as an utmost challenge by most, skillful time management. He introduces what it will take, exactly how to prepare your strategies, and how to stay focused and prioritize tasks once you have laid out and are ready to implement all your steps. The concept of working in chunks is a life changer, and has enabled me to tackle issues and tasks I have not dared to commence in years! The book certainly ignited a definite can-do attitude in me, and my motivation has sky-rocketed. What a relief to finally feel truly in control of one's own time! Whether you are an entrepreneur, a corporate executive, a doctor, or a stay-at-home parent, the strategies are clearly laid out and implementable by everyone, and you will be happy to always have this book to fall back on as reference!

Evren Tore, *Retired banker (United Kingdom)*

The book connects the dots to what was discussed in other programs by Dr Sundardas and provides a foundation to time management. It gave me greater clarity and also made me realize the importance of preparation and planning to time management. The concepts put forth are easily digested by the reader and steps are thoughtful and concise. I started to plan each work day using those steps and they help me be focused. The plans are not perfect and am still tweaking but it led me to understand the importance of being focus in achieving the tasks. I also noticed the state of my body condition also determines the level of my productivity each day, thereby reinforcing the importance of building up my tanks.

Jolene Koh, *Compliance Manager (Singapore)*

This book has been an amazing resource that leaves no stone unturned in the challenging area of time management. It not only breaks the steps for managing time down into clear detailed parts, it also addresses so many roadblocks that get in the way and provides strategies to deal with them. To top it off, the information is masterfully distilled and presented simply and clearly such that it is accessible to all. It is no doubt a book worth returning to again and again until hopefully mastery is achieved!

Bay Chern Chieh, *Homeschooling Mother (Singapore)*

Other Books by Sundardas D Annamalay

1. The Asian Woman's Guide to Health, Beauty and Vitality
2. Awakening the Genius in your Child
3. Maximize your Child's Emotional Intelligence
4. The Science of Healing Waters
5. Water – The Untold Story
6. Every Woman's Guide to Vitality and Anti-Ageing
7. Art and Science of Vibrational Medicine
8. Out Front (co-author)
9. Protecting Yourself and Your Family Against Radiation Toxicity
10. Are You the Missing Piece? (co-author)

https://youtu.be/veu64nAfcE0

INTRODUCTION

We all have things to do, people to see and targets to hit. Many of us either run our own businesses or work for others. If there is one thing that we could have more of apart from money it's time. In fact, since the advent of the Industrial Revolution, as access to information and ease of communication started speeding up, we have found ourselves with less and less time.

The neurosis of modern civilization is clock time. We are seeing more people getting sick and dying, more divorces and failed relationships, more alienation of the young because we have lost control of time.

Many of my clients and patients have struggles involving relationships, achieving targets, and even being able to sleep. Others struggle to develop new habits to support their new life goals and ambitions. At the heart of all their struggles is an uneasy relationship with priorities and resource allocation.

I have long been fascinated by how people use their energy. I have always looked at cutting-edge ways to do things more easily. My calendar has always been chock full of things to do and targets to hit. I thought I had worked out a very good energy-management system.

However, as time went on, I began to realize I was working harder and harder but feeling less and less effective. Many of my strategies and methods were becoming less productive. I wonder if you have ever felt this way too? This led me to review some ground-breaking research around time management and what neuroscience has to say about how our brain processes time as we grow older and how we process time as we become more stressed.

After almost thirty years of feeling I had an effective time management system, I reached the limits of what I knew. As the number of companies I was running and the complexity of the projects I was involved in grew, I realized that a brand-new approach was called for. I could no longer repeat the same old tired strategies.

I became aware that most people did not value their time enough. They often did not use their time in fruitful and effective ways. Also, at different times in our lives, as we go through life cycle changes, our priorities and values change as well. This would dramatically impact our relationship with time and productivity. Simply trying to squeeze more into the day would no longer work, or be effective. We had to learn to focus on higher-ticket items in our lives and businesses.

So from all these perceptions and the experience of working with more than 15,000 individuals, a new model of time management was born. This model includes the latest findings in neuroscience, concepts in systems thinking, and meditative practices as well as concepts familiar to energy management. The graduates of my programs have long asked me to formally put all these concepts together.

With this model of time management, you will begin to understand your personal, day-to-day time rhythms as well as the life cycles that you move through. You will learn about the value of your time, and what you can do to increase this value. As you do so, you will find you are doing more and more in less and less time, easily and effortlessly.

Welcome to Mastering Time. Discover how to tune into your innate natural rhythms so that you can ride on your cycles of positive energy. Discover the best ways to use your resources and energy so that you maximize the use of your time while minimizing stress. Learn the secrets of successful people: how they live healthy, productive, and profitable lives. Real time management will add years to your life, and life to your years. What is more, you will enjoy life even more.

Welcome to **Life by Design: Mastering Energy, Money and Leverage in 9 Simple Steps**.

https://youtu.be/RC8CrE1GoUc

1

WHY PRIORITISE?

*What then is time? If no one asks me, I know what it is. If
I wish to explain it to him who asks, I do not know.*

Saint Augustine

"If only I had more resources…"

How often have you heard yourself say that? If you are like most people
living in the twenty-first century, pretty often! Of course we know we
cannot create twenty-five hours for the day, or an eighth day for the
week. Managing resources for better results has become an amazingly
sought-after activity among people everywhere. There are endless
motives to manage time for greater productivity, which is why lots of
people choose to attempt it.

Some people start managing their energy to become more productive
and efficient. Others do so to experience peace of mind, or to have a
more fulfilling life. Although the motives for managing time and energy
for greater productivity are endless, there are several that stick out as
the most significant.

Why are some people able to quickly grow their business or advance
their careers while others work equally hard but can never really make
the forward progress they know they are capable of? Why is it that
some people continue to fall deeper and deeper in love with their spouse
and maintain a powerful connection with their kids while others find

themselves growing more and more distant in their most important relationships?

And how is it that some people always seem to have an abundance of energy, constantly traveling to beautiful places, living a fascinating life full of contribution and meaning, and busy learning and teaching? And others are stuck in an endless loop of complaining and blaming because they find themselves drifting through life, swept up in a daily routine they never imagined living.

Well, I am about to show you. And I am about to show you how, if you want, you can make the next year your best year ever.

How you prioritize will determine your eventual future. The key is to zero in on your core priority, and design a lean, efficient life plan that leaves you fulfilled and satisfied. This is when less becomes a lot more.

As a downstream effect, you end up being more productive. It may seem counter-intuitive to spend time learning about how to prioritize so that you can save time, energy, and resources. However, when done well, the benefits are enormous:

- Increased opportunities both personal and professional
- Better professional reputation
- Enhanced career advancement
- Reduced Stress

Managing your priorities badly can have very undesirable consequences:

- Inefficient workflow
- Poor work quality
- Reduced career advancement prospects
- Greater stress

Become Very Productive and Efficient

Prioritizing properly — to achieve greater productivity and efficiency, so as to live a more fulfilling life — provides a great rationale. Every time you have a well-specified rationale to manage time for greater productivity, it makes your aspirations more meaningful. Then when you are finally successfully managing a day at work, it feels most fulfilling. You can set yourself up to have the most extraordinary year of your life.

That can mean reaching new levels financially in your business, or making major advancements in your career. It can mean reconnecting or reviving a meaningful relationship that's lost its spark or now feels distant. It can also mean getting into the best shape of your life physically, mentally, and emotionally.

But it can also mean having a far greater impact in life: contributing to your church or community, involving yourself in a cause you are passionate about.

If you have ever felt like you were capable of more but weren't sure on how get from here to there, or if you knew deep down that there was this enormous potential below the surface of your life but something kept getting in the way, then you are in the right place.

Or maybe you are already a high performer and take pride in your ability to achieve, but you are starting to realize that your success in one area is costing you in other areas such as your family, your health, or maybe even your mental wellbeing.

Have the date nights with your spouse dropped off? Is your passion fading? Your kids just assume that you won't be at their soccer games or dance recitals because you are likely to be too busy to attend?

I say this because I have been there. And it's easy to try and justify it by just saying "Well, it's just a busy season and once we get this next project out the door things will slow down." But if we are truly being honest with each other, you and I know the real truth: things never just slow down, right?

How Being Compulsive Can Trip You Up

Once a compulsive person reaches one level of success he immediately sets his sights on the next. Well, I was such a guy. And later on, you'll hear how this compulsion nearly caused me my health, my business, and my relationship with my family. But here is the good news: if you have gotten derailed from accomplishing what you set out to achieve, or you have an ambitious goal that you want to finally commit to next year, this book is going to give you the foundation you need to make massive progress over the next twelve months.

The focus of this book is to reveal how you can stop feeling overwhelmed, accomplish what matters most, and finally realize your potential. And there is no better time than now to set the stage for your success over the next twelve months.

Plus, I'm going to help you design a life that works, so you are able to say "Yes" to the things that matter — and eliminate everything else that slows you down. The clearer you can be about how to organize your daily life to support your bigger vision, the more you'll step into your true potential, stay on track, and accomplish all that you want and deserve. Are you ready to make that happen?

Now before we dig in, I've got to warn you about something that's critically important. And believe me not paying attention to this will virtually guarantee another wasted year.

You may be thinking that what I am about to share with you is just another spin on goal setting.

Oh, you know I have tried that before and it didn't work for me.

I am already good at setting and achieving goals.

Stop. This is so much deeper than goal setting. The last thing I want is for you to think that just by writing down your goals on a napkin at a New Year's Eve party, or announcing your resolutions on Facebook at the beginning of the year, that you'll magically accomplish big goals. You and I both know that thinking is flawed; the statistics prove it.

Did you know that 25 percent of people abandon their New Year's resolutions after just one week? That 60 percent give up within six months? It's the same reason the average person makes the same New Year's Resolution *ten separate times without success*. I am not here to give you false hope. I am here to share a proven process that will help you design your best year ever.

So how do others make significant progress in their life? Well I can promise you this: it is not because they are smarter, or they have some mysterious secret power (though I know it can feel like that).

The kind of progress I'm speaking about doesn't *just* happen. To get from where you are to where you want to go takes the right intention plus an effective plan. The people around you who keep winning and achieving? They are not special — they simply know how to set themselves up for success.

They have the right foundation, the right mind set, and the right system to consistently get what they want. They've learned how to avoid getting stuck on the urgent matters, and instead follow a fool-proof process that allows them to stay focused on the stuff that really matters.

Lose sight of what's important — and that family vacation you've been meaning to take gets pushed back for another year, that fitness regimen never gets started. And worst of all, it means the commitments you've made to prioritize your family and your health all get pushed down the list because they aren't urgent.

The urgent is something we've all grown to despise. It distracts you, interrupts you, and somehow finds a way to take priority over the things that matter most in your life. It doesn't care about your intentions for meaningful progress. It doesn't care what you want. It's selfish. It wants what it wants when it wants it.

And it always comes at a cost to you and to those around you. It means that book you've always wanted to write doesn't get written. It means that friend you have been meaning to call doesn't get called.

What Happens When You Don't Manage Your Priorities?

Managing your priorities properly will allow you to have longevity in your results. The following facts are based on US statistics.

- There will be two million marriages in the USA this year and one million divorces.
- 95 percent of divorces are caused by a "lack of communication".
- The average working person spends less than two minutes per day in meaningful communication with their spouse or "significant other".
- The average working person spends less than thirty seconds a day talking to their children.

These statistics reflect people who did not make their marriage or their relationships with their kids their number one priority.

Many people will spend more time on choosing a car, picking a dress, or planning for a holiday than they will on improving their marriage, improving communication with their partner, or communicating with their children.

There were 2.5 million deaths in the USA in 2014. 75 percent were from causes that were largely preventable:*

1) **Obesity**
2) **Alcohol**
3) **Smoking**

* CDC report: http://www.cdc.gov/nchs/

All the above revolve around priorities and habits and how people have become habituated to spend their time. They have literally "chosen" to spend their time on death-dealing activities over fifteen to forty years.

Do any of the situations below sound familiar?

- Missing deadlines, feelings of constant rushing
- Indecision about taking action, time spent on non-productive activity
- Feeling overwhelmed, fatigued or listless
- Not enough time for things that you like to do or for family and friends
- Facing the day without plans or goals, feeling distracted from the important things.

If so, you may benefit from the better ways of managing your core priorities we present in the pages that follow.

Food Habits and Programming

Studies by experts at St. Georges University, London, have proven a link between teenage consumption of sugary drinks and impulses towards fatty and salty foods. They found that the stomach's gut lining absorbed these food types more quickly and activated the brain's pleasure center quickly. The brain then also dampened its impulses for the intake of vitamins and minerals. These cravings or impulses driven by the brain create an addictive effect: addiction to sugary drinks and salty or fatty foods.

Other UK research on rats has shown that sugar is as addictive to the brain as cocaine, and sugar intake plays a role in the creation of addictive impulses in humans.

Adults do not suffer significant sugar-addiction withdrawal symptoms; children, however, have been found to react more strongly, getting more intense withdrawal symptoms. Tantrums, restlessness, sweats, and distracted attention are noted behaviors. Longer-term studies are underway to explore the implications of these observations and findings.

Fruit and sports-energy drinks are not excepted from this category: many have higher sugar levels than some fizzy drinks, and also may also contain addictive amounts of caffeine and related substances. Studies show that the benefits, sporting or health-wise, to consumers from both these classes of drinks are more marketing hype than real. Weight gain was determined as being the only likely outcome.

The other main concern about all these categories of drinks is the corrosive impact they have on children's and adults' teeth. Studies by dentists as reported in the UK British Dental Journal as well as the USA Oral Hygiene Journal both noted findings about colas (soft drinks) and citric acids in drinks.

They noted that citric acid, which is a common 'tangy' ingredient in all these drinks, increased the risk of tooth erosion by 252 percent, and that cola drinks are ten times as corrosive as fruit juice in the first three minutes of teeth contact, respectively.

Many USA-based health organizations are reviewing the research and are calling for regulation as well as a review of all the drinks-industry guidelines. Medical groups are linking the obesity crisis in the western world in part to the habit-forming roles around food and diet that soft drinks play in shaping the health outcomes of recent generations. Obesity is the new smoking crisis in these circles.

The average adult woman is supposed to have a daily intake of ninety grams of sugar in her diet while a man can absorb 120 grams per day.

Children are supposed to have a far lower intake. Many soft and fruit drinks provide that daily intake in one can or bottle.

The images of happiness, fun, and health which dominate the marketing themes of the drinks industry are not supported by the research findings emerging from numerous types of studies being conducted on human health. These billion-dollar industries are not likely to change their products or admit concerns willingly.

Coca Cola paid Olympic organizers more than one hundred million pounds to become the official provider of soft drinks to the Olympics. The association between health and sporting achievement on one hand, and soft drinks on the other hand, becomes entrenched by such opportunities. The burden on regulating these drinks falls on families and individuals.

The role of emotions and stress in creating the impulse for sugary food and drink intake is also revealed by several studies. In body-mind science, we note that addictions and emotional issues including depression seem to accompany sugar cravings in many people. A soft drink can be an easily-obtained crutch when the impulse strikes.

The answer lies in education and discipline. The declining mental, emotional, and physical health of wider and wider cross-sections of the population has some of its roots in our choice of foods and drinks.

We should be mindful of our choices. For instance, the assumption that sugary drinks offer any benefit or are harmless choices for ourselves and our children, is simply programming we got as a child — and there are several others, pertaining to food, that we received. This is true about food; now think about the conditioning about the work ethic, being able to say "No", etc., that we were also subjected to.

Then one day you wake up asking yourself "Where does this extra ten or twenty kilos come from?", "Why am I finding it difficult to love my spouse?", "Why am I living here or in this job?", or "Why do I feel like something is missing?"

Well if you can relate to any of this, I have got good news: you're normal. It doesn't however have to stay this way.

I have developed a process to improve how I prioritize and use my energy and time. As you'll soon see, I had to. When I started using this process year after year, my life, in all areas — career, relationships, health — completely took a turn for the better. I became more alive mentally, emotionally, and spiritually; I began having a far greater impact than I ever had before.

Planning

Begin with the end in mind. Planning in advance helps you manage life for greater productivity. Understandably, it may be difficult to get into the practice of doing so. Begin by planning each day, and it will become force of habit when you manage time for longer intervals in the future.

People who elect to manage their life for better results are very determined. There are lots of things in life that can't be faked. You can't fake a job evaluation, or the outcome of an exam in college.

Similarly, you can't fake managing priorities for greater productivity. You simply can't manage time effectively without a little preparation. It takes focus and determination for an individual to manage his priorities for a fulfilling life.

If all this is not your cup of tea, you will find yourself becoming more and more reluctant at the idea of starting. That is not necessarily bad. You have just discovered that you are not cut out to do a time-management program on your own.

For everyone who recognizes that he could manage time better and does something about this, there are about ninety others who are either in denial or have dreamy ideas of becoming better organized in the distant future. Whether you are looking at managing a day at work or years of your life successfully, there are steps you can take to realize your objectives.

Preparation takes time and must not be rushed. By scurrying through the preparation stage, you will not truly be preparing. Designing your life for greater productivity is exciting, and grants a sense of achievement that you will appreciate for years. Good Life Design can be a real challenge. Whether you are a newbie or a seasoned pro, there are rational pros and cons of effective Life Design. The top advantage of Life Design for greater productivity is that it will allow you a sense of pride and achievement.

It is vital to realize that although you may have an intellectual appreciation for the benefits of a well-crafted life plan, this alone is insufficient. Unless and until you have an emotional need and an appreciation for the benefits of having more time, energy, and resources in your life, you are unlikely to do anything about prioritizing well. Life Design for a fulfilling life is a challenging activity.

Another benefit of Life Design is that it perfects your organizational skills as you map out how you will move forward to ultimately managing a day at work or years of your life successfully. So as soon as you elect to manage time, you begin to learn about planning and staying focused.

There are indisputable benefits to Life Design for greater productivity. It is however not as painless as it seems. There may be certain restrictions that you possibly have to get over, like the investment of time, energy, and commitment required to plan and execute.

You need to make a steadfast commitment. Do not attempt to plan erratically. Devotion along with sincere efforts will eventually lead you to managing a day at work successfully.

Life Design for greater productivity needs an individual to become focused, relentless, and even enlightened. When you view yourself as the kind of person with these virtues, you are totally ready to manage a day at work successfully. The most essential thing to be mindful of is that there are no shortcuts.

Have A Fulfilled Life

Another reason that people choose to manage time is to have a fulfilled life.

While doing so can be challenging, the rewards can be significant. We make the most of the time that we have; not just do we achieve much more but also we can significantly reduce stress. Usually when a person considers improving how he lives, he does so because he is experiencing extreme dissatisfaction or chaos, or feeling overwhelmed. If you are one of those, congratulations! You are ripe for change, you are clearly serious about changing, and you have just what you need: this book.

Priority and energy management done well is a gift to yourself: the gift of feeling more in control of your life. This is because "time management" is really "priority and energy management". It's about spending less time in non-productive ways that leave you feeling rushed and frustrated. It's about putting your focus on what you truly value. Maybe you will even be able to schedule relaxation.

What Are Your Priorities?

You can think of this book as doing for your life and career what a professional housekeeper will do for your shoe rack.

My step-daughter kept complaining there was no room for her shoes. She kept buying shoes. Some she used, some she did not, some needed to be repaired. She kept everything, thinking that she might need them one day. Finally, the matter got totally out of control, and she decided to clean it up and sort it out. She kept the shoes she used regularly, the shoes she looked good in. She sold the shoes she never used at a thrift store. She looked at the shoes that needed to be fixed, realized she would never fix them, and threw them away.

You need both discipline and a system, otherwise you end up either keeping all the shoes or giving or throwing away the ones you later discover you need. In exactly the same way, our life gets cluttered with commitments and activities that were well-intended. Most of these have no expiry dates, so we never stop doing them unless we develop a system for eliminating them.

Are you clear about your priorities in life, relationships, health, and career? The reality is only one really matters — your life must revolve around only one major priority. You have to decide. You have to pick the one priority that that will help you grow and thrive and keep it all together. Once you have that, the other pieces come together. This is how someone determined to live the "Life by Design" would approach it.

Key Points to DESIGN YOUR LIFE

Prioritizing, planning, and scheduling is the process by which you design your life. By doing so you can reduce your stress levels and maximize your effectiveness.

---

9 STEPS TO "LIFE BY DESIGN"

1) **Decide on the essential priorities necessary for you to succeed in your job/business/life.**
2) **Identify the time/resources you have available.**
3) **Identify what goals and targets you need to achieve.**
4) **Identify what is irrelevant, intrusive, and drains energy.**
5) **Eliminate habits and behaviors and commitments that do not serve you.**
6) **Create firewalls to protect your boundaries and learn to say "No" to what doesn't serve you.**
7) **Schedule the goals and targets you need to achieve (develop your prioritized To-Do List).**
8) **Ensure that you have the right habits in place to achieve your targets.**
9) **Execute your plan and correct your course.**

A) EVALUATE

Instead of asking, "Is there a chance I will wear this pair of shoes sometime in the future?", ask yourself the tough questions. "Do I absolutely love this pair of shoes?", "Do I wear this often?", "Do I look fabulous wearing this pair of shoes?" If the answer is no, you know that you have to throw that pair away.

In your personal and professional life, the equivalent question is "Will this activity contribute significantly to my personal and professional life?" Part 1 of this book addresses this question.

1) **Decide on the essential priorities necessary for you to succeed in your job/business/life.**
2) **Identify the time/resources you have available.**
3) **Identify what goals and targets you need to achieve.**

B) DISCARD

Let's say you divide your shoes into different piles: the shoes you use regularly; the shoes you look good in; the shoes that you never use; and the shoes that need to be fixed but which you know you are never going to fix. You keep the shoes you want on the shoe rack. The rest you put into two bags. One bag is for what you can sell at the thrift store. The other is for the ones you deliberately choose to throw away.

In other words, it is not enough to identify which activities don't significantly contribute to your life. You still must actively eliminate the activities that do not contribute. Part 2 of the book addresses this question.

4) **Identify what is irrelevant, intrusive, and drains energy.**
5) **Eliminate habits and behaviors and commitments that do not serve you.**
6) **Create firewalls to protect your boundaries and learn to say no to what doesn't serve you.**

C) IMPLEMENT

If you want your shoe rack to stay tidy, you need to regularly repeat the decluttering process. There are shoes that you keep on the shoe rack, shoes that you take to the thrift store, and the broken-down shoes you're going to dump. How do you turn this process into a routine you do automatically and regularly?

How do you implement activities that contribute significantly to your personal and professional life and create routines so they are automatic? Part 3 of the book addresses this question.

7) **Schedule the goals and targets you need to achieve (develop your prioritized To-Do List).**
8) **Ensure that you have the right habits in place to achieve your targets.**
9) **Execute your life plan and correct your course.**

Compulsive Life	Designed Life
I can do it all	I can do it all but not at the same time
I can prioritize my life	I have only one major priority
I make commitments enthusiastically	I honor all commitments required

A) EVALUATE

Identify The Difference That Makes The Difference

One of my seminar participants once accused me of making life "boring" by insisting on prioritizing and planning. She felt that she wanted to be in the moment and be spontaneous. It took her a few years before she realized that you can be truly spontaneous only when you have a disciplined approach, developed core skills, and then set time aside for spontaneity.

So in order to understand what really matters to you, you need to explore and evaluate. Those who eventually become crystal clear about what matters do so because they have the benefit of hindsight, experience, and evidence that something really works for them.

To explore all that is relevant and possible, you need a base from which you can narrow down what is clearly the core for you, the crucial "difference" that makes the difference. You have to explore and evaluate a broad range of possibilities in depth before you can conclude about what really works. So you need to test things out in small ways before committing in a big way to what matters to you.

Contrast this approach with many Singaporeans who finish school, go to college then polytechnic or university, then go out into the workforce. They know nothing about what truly matters in their personal, emotional or professional lives. They accept conventional perspectives about what is important. Then in their late thirties or forties they start struggling with overwhelming doubt. In private conversations in my office they often plaintively ask me, "What is my life purpose?"

If you believe, as I did when I was living my "Compulsive Life", that being driven and being overly busy was a sign of productivity, you also believe that creating the space and time to think, explore, and reflect is a luxury. Yet, these very activities are the cure to the curse of focusing on trivialities while missing the core issues in your life. They are crucial for identifying the difference that makes the difference.

Dedicated "Life Designers" spend significant chunks of time exploring, questioning, arguing, and thinking. The purpose of the exploration is to hone in on what truly matters. To focus on the difference that makes the difference.

A) EVALUATE

1) Decide on the essential priorities necessary for you to succeed in your job/business/life.

https://youtu.be/ZZAlWWlERFY

2

DESIGN YOUR LIFE

Know the true value of time; snatch, seize, and enjoy every moment of it. No idleness, no laziness, no procrastination: never put off till tomorrow what you can do today.

Philip Stanhope, 4th Earl of Chesterfield

We live in a time of incredible opportunity. Never before have we had the opportunity to architect or engineer our lives, and then have the agency and resources to make it a reality. It's such an exciting time, and this book can help: it will demystify the process of getting what you want and put you on the fast track to designing the life you are made for.

When I implemented the principles in this book, my clients noticed the significant changes and asked me what I was doing. So I shared what I'd done with a few people. What I found was that they were all looking for the same thing: clarity. Clarity on what they needed to do to get themselves going in the right direction, and, most importantly, clarity on how to stay on track.

That is why I wrote this book, and that is why I expanded these concepts into "Life by Design: Mastering Energy, Money and Leverage in 9 Simple Steps".

Before I outline the core foundational elements of this process, it's important to know where they came from. The seeds of this were planted many, many years ago.

Growing up as a young boy I loved reading and figuring things out. I dreamed about the things I wanted to explore and the machines I wanted to create. I was a regular geek.

And all through my adolescence and early teens there was one person in particular whom I could rely on to keep my life stable. You probably have a person like this in your life. Someone who so long as he or she is there, life as you know it will go on.

Picture that person in your mind right now. And now let me ask you a question. Is there anything worse than when this person lets you down? Well, that's what happened to me. It's not worth going into the details here, and you probably have a similar story of your own, but I'll say this: I counted on this person for everything and one day I realized I couldn't.

The person who was supposed to always be there was no longer there. She checked out, and in a big way. I was crushed. It was not her fault. That did not change things. It was my mother. She got very sick and in a year and half she died of cancer.

Crushed as I was, I was also determined. I made a silent vow in my heart: "I will never depend on anyone else again." I didn't realize it at the time but that vow became the driving force of my life.

And here is the truth: I overcorrected, I way overcorrected. It seems that the next morning I cut my hair, put on a suit and got a job. I wanted control because it felt like everything in my life was suddenly out of control.

I started my own business after I completed my training as a naturopathic physician. I was full of myself, but I was also in control, and there was a broken part of me that needed that.

Then I got married. I was working on my postgraduate degrees, running my business, and looking after my step-son. Everyone around me was telling me it was not possible to do so much, so quickly, but I wanted to prove them wrong.

Life got stressful and fast. Providing for a family and trying to build a business was tough. I got so wrapped up in my drive to succeed that soon the one thing I didn't want to happen to me was happening.

I was not measuring up. Now I became the person who was not measuring up. My wife and I went through marital challenges. Eventually, even as the business began to succeed, my marriage fell apart. This happens very often to compulsive people.

Well, up to that point my life had demonstrated two unhelpful ways of approaching life. I call the first one "Coasting Along". That was how my father approached life. He was swept up in the current, coasting along, not choosing his destination and ending up in a place he never would have chosen if he had consciously been aware of it. He was pulled in a hundred different directions and whichever pulled hardest was the focus for the day, week or month. And that, I had decided, was exactly how I was never going to live my life.

Unfortunately, that's how a lot of people approach life. They just operate automatically. They are caught up in life's distractions. They don't think about where they might be going, and before long they end up at a destination they would not have chosen if they were conscious of what they were choosing. The unintended destination may be a health crisis, a marital crisis, a business failure, or a career upset; whatever it is, they end up in a place far from what they thought they were going.

But the alternative — that's where I was, and you may be there too — is what I call "The Compulsive Life". This is the overcorrection to "Coasting Along". This is the type of person that takes great pride in setting and achieving goals. They are hyper-driven on making progress. But this person is so driven at excelling in one area of their life that they often neglect the other areas, and that's what happened to me. You ignore, until it is too late, whatever does not contribute to your goals. And if you are not careful, it can lead to the destruction of important relationships, your health, and a lot more. We get so rewarded for being successful and appreciated for being 'On time, on target' that we keep doing more and more.

Before we go any further I want to underline something. In neither approach was the person doing destructive things intentionally. What's interesting is that "Coasting Along" and "The Compulsive Life" are really two sides of the same coin. They may seem like polar opposites, but they have more in common than you may think.

Firstly, both these approaches are largely unconscious approaches to life. Secondly, both will take you to destinations you would never consciously choose. Both are often characterized by feeling that you are being pulled in different directions. Both will end up using your energies in ways you never intended. Both will lead to unintended consequences. I call this the Option A choice (see image below).

Option A

Each little edge represents another priority that sucks energy, another commitment that you will struggle to keep and feel guilty about for failing, something that will wear you down until you hit burnout or worse.

Thankfully, there is a third alternative, what I call "Life by Design", which leads to a life of freedom. This is a life of being conscious of choosing a destination, developing a plan, and following a proven process that ensures we get there. It doesn't mean there won't be detours. It does mean living intentionally and giving ourselves every advantage we can to stay on track and succeed both in business and in life. I call this the Option B choice, or Life by Design. There is only one major priority (see image below).

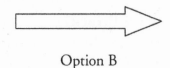

Option B

How are you living now? Are you spending your time the way you want to? Or are you at the mercy of forces outside your control?

Now, the way to start living a more designed life with known destinations and wanted outcomes is by asking and answering critical questions. Your answers to these questions will provide the foundation on which you build everything else.

Before I had clear answers to these questions my work consumed me. I was constantly stressed. I was present for my business but absent from everything else. Yes, I eventually developed a business that became very financially successful. But outside of that, my life was a mess. I made some improvements but they were just cosmetic. My marriage crashed and I experienced several serious health concerns.

Now fast forward to today. The "Life by Design" process has completely revived my career, my relationships, and my health. I am having more impact helping more people now than ever before.

This process has kept me from getting side-tracked, and it's given me the freedom to breathe and enjoy life. Financially, I am making more, running more businesses than before. And most importantly, my life is way less stressful.

Common reasons for doing time-management programs are to experience peace of mind, be more prepared for the unexpected, and have a smoother ride through life. These are all excellent reasons to manage time.

Personal Experience Of Priorities

Let me give you an example of my own priorities. My first priority today is me. But it didn't use to be.

The truth is that if you don't exercise appropriate self-care you're not going to be of any use to anybody. For example, if you don't deal with your emotional baggage then you are going to drag that into any relationship you have. If you don't take care of yourself physically (which applied to me at one point), you are asking for something serious like a heart attack or some other health crisis.

Some health issues can't be avoided; I get that. Nevertheless, as we all know, a lot of health issues are self-inflicted. An appropriate level of self-care is vital if you want to lead a rewarding life and have the resources you need to truly serve others.

My succeeding priorities are my wife, my children, and then my work. My work is way down the list because I know that my work will flourish when I have a rich personal life.

Years ago, when I was living "The Compulsive Life", my priorities weren't in this order. But going through the "Life By Design" process, starting with asking questions, I made an important discovery which contradicts a lot of people who say you can win at business or you can win at life but you can't win at both.

But here is my contrary experience: you can't win at one without winning at the other. Success means both. Don't let the urgent take precedence over the important. Don't convince yourself that the situation you are now in is temporary. Why? Because temporary things have a way of first becoming permanent and then becoming a lifestyle. So don't just drift along or drive compulsively. Take the third path, ask the third question: "What commitment will I make now to achieve my ideal future?"

A few years ago, before I formalized "Life by Design", I was working on my schedule for the forthcoming year. I thought I had a well-thought-out plan, but remembered that one year earlier I had had the same thought but had grossly over-committed myself. So I looked at my plan again, estimated the number of hours needed to achieve it, and realized that I had under-estimated the time and resources I required. I needed 500 more hours to achieve that plan.

That was a major wake-up call. I felt really desperate because so many things — the current businesses, future projects, my staff — were riding on me. I felt exhausted. I thought there had to be another way.

And there was. It took three months to reconfigure everything. It took another six months to change and implement all the ways of thinking about managing time, energy, and resources that I had been doing for the last forty years. Once I did, and got everyone in my companies on board, everything changed.

Suddenly I had time to exercise almost every day, and go on movie dates with my wife once a month instead of twice a year. Plus, my companies became more profitable.

So often we make a mountain out of a molehill; this loss of perspective can be disastrous over a long period of time. And it really comes down to making that one single commitment. So let me ask you this right now. As we've been talking about this, you have probably been thinking of a commitment you need to make, right? Maybe it's a tough conversation you need to have. Maybe it's an action you need to take. What is it for you? What's the thing that's going to move the needle?

Your decision may push you outside of your comfort zone, but listen: *all the important stuff happens outside your comfort zone.* If you feel uncomfortable just thinking about this, fantastic! Embrace it. That's right where you should be. Nothing really changes inside the comfort zone.

What is the next single commitment you need to make, if you want to live a life by design, if you want to be courageous, if you don't want to live by default, if you don't want to be in overdrive?

Before embarking on a time- and energy-management program, you ought to decide if this is a suitable choice for you. If you cannot give up television time, surfing the Internet endlessly, or chatting on your Facebook account, this may not be for you. The easiest method to make this assessment would be to ask yourself the following distinct questions:

- What is the number one priority in your life?
- Do you want to achieve more with less effort?
- Do you want to have a higher quality of life?
- Are you prepared to spend one hour a day organizing your life so that you can plan at the beginning of the day and reflect at the end on how you did?

I hope you are clear about your answers to the above questions. These same questions are asked by everyone who is motivated to make more of his life. You have now taken the first step towards managing resources for greater productivity!

Life Design takes more than getting up one afternoon and saying, "Oh, I need to manage my time to live life well." Sure, that is a necessary starting step; you must always first invest in yourself mentally. Overall, designing your life will bring a huge sense of achievement to you. Also, preparing for this is a stimulating undertaking, which is the real reason that some people elect to start.

Life Design also gives you a new outlook on things. As soon as you manage your time better, you begin to recognize that you can accomplish just about anything in this world. You become clearer about what the important things in life are about.

Motivations for managing time are different from one individual to another; ensure your reasons are clear to you.

Identify The Difference That Makes The Difference

What if we can seize control of our lives instead of being at the mercy of a media that encourages conspicuous consumption? What if we choose to do only what adds meaning and value to our lives, the lives of our families, and communities?

Everything changes when we accept accountability for our lives, when we exercise our freedom to choose wisely and well. We can ascend to the next level of achievement and growth in our lives when we replace what we find trivial with what makes the vital difference. We are no longer trapped in other people's agendas. We are free to make meaningful choices.

What if instead of buying more stuff, we focused on creating more space to think, breathe, and be? What if we stopped trying so hard to make money we don't need, to buy things we don't want, to impress people we don't really care about?

What if we stopped measuring our progress in life by how busy we are? Instead, we measured it by how much time we spent meditating, pondering, communicating, and enjoying time with the most important people in our lives. How would we live differently?

I have always been acutely aware of how little time I have and how limited my energy and resources are. So I need to make sure that I use my time and energy optimally to make a difference to myself, my family, and my community.

I had the time to reflect on the meaning of my life when I had a near-death experience when I was about forty-two. Years from now, when I reach the same point again, I want to make sure I have no regrets about how I spent my time after that near-death experience. What about you?

The table below outlines the difference between the Compulsive Life model doing standard time-management techniques and the Designed Life model.

Compulsive Life	Designed Life
I have unlimited energy	I have limited energy and resources
I make life choices in the moment	I choose deliberately
I respond to whatever comes up	I stay with my priority
I will seize every opportunity	I will not be detracted from my priority

https://youtu.be/ZdH6_tC6Rcs

3

WHAT ARE THE MIND TRAPS THAT BLIND YOU?

To see a World in a Grain of Sand
And a Heaven in a Wild Flower
Hold Infinity in the palm of your hand
And Eternity in an hour…

William Blake, **Auguries of Innocence**

As a poet, philosopher, and mystic, I remain fascinated by these words. As a physician, scientist, and businessman the above lines spell "Danger".

Paul Mclean popularized the concept of the *Triune Brain*. While neuroscience has since moved on, the Triune-Brain concept is a very useful model for understanding how the brain functions:

Instinctual / Reptilian: This is the Seat of the Reticular Activating System (RAS). This part of your brain automatically makes meaning out of what happens. Most deep-seated programs involving fundamental survival reside here, including programming about safety, security, and money.

Limbic / Emotional: This part of your brain connects with your emotions. All your decisions are emotional in nature. Your emotions help you choose and make choices. It is also the seat of the *amygdala*, the part of your "emotional brain" that works to keep you safe. It restricts or reduces your choices so that you are 'safe'. Your beliefs run this area. At the best of times your beliefs limit your freedom of choice.

Neo-Cortex / Thinking: The only part of the brain where you can make conscious choice.

Every day I meet clients who struggle with challenges in their lives because they fail to recognize the reality confronting them. Very commonly they have mental filters and blinkers and emotional triggers that distort what they see, hear, and feel.

Some of these processes are useful in a given context. Out of that context they became downright dangerous. These processes include:

1) **Deletion: Your brain has to make sense of thousands of stimuli per second. So after a while it screens out repeated background "details". There are also things you don't want to see or hear because they make you uncomfortable, so you screen them out as well.**

As a result, you don't pay attention to your loved one when they are struggling with a real problem, and get shocked when they get a heart attack and drop dead.

You don't pay attention to how your client is presenting himself/herself and you miss vital clues that could help you close the sale. You kiss a thousand dollars goodbye.

2) **Generalization: You have always done it a certain way, so you conclude that is the only way.**

Something happened enough times in your life with enough intensity to create a neural pathway in your brain. So you concluded that "Love hurts" because some people you were close to died or left. You saw enough examples of unethical behavior by rich people so you concluded that "Rich people are bad people."

You do not pay attention to the changes in the environment or people. You fail to recognize major changes in the environment that would invalidate a certain marketing or business approach. Your business dips 20 percent because you missed the trend.

If you are lucky, your wife smiles sweetly at you (while she quietly curses) because you bought her a gift identical to what her best friend is wearing. (You were not keeping track.) In the long term, these little things wear your business and your relationships down.

3) **Distortion: This process is the basis for creativity. It creates great artist and poets — like Picasso and his Cubist style of painting — who do creative things with their imagination. On the other hand, it can also lead to major issues. One person's model of accuracy is another's model of obsessive-compulsive attention to detail.**
4) **Projection: Whatever secret fears and anxieties you have, you deny having them. You ascribe it to the people around you. You are an anxious person but you cannot accept it. Your cab driver looks at you and asks you if everything is fine and you conclude your cab driver is anxious.**

So the processes of deletion, distortion, and generalization, and to a lesser extent projection, will determine what we allow into our world. In that sense, they are filters. They end up forming our values, biases, and beliefs.

At the same time, based on these processes we will also design a future where all our biases, beliefs, and values are validated. If that is so you cannot design a future that is appreciably different from the past.

Based on these processes, you design on an unconscious basis a story (script) about yourself. After a while, this script is so much a part of you and so real to you that you call it "Your Real Life Story". It has become a self-fulfilling prophecy.

I will henceforth refer to all these stories, your automatic patterns of behavior both good and bad, as "Default Modes" or DMs. Why? Because when you do not think or reflect, or you are in a state of arousal or depression, you will revert to these default modes (DMs).

After thirty-five years of age, you have only five minutes of willpower or choice in a day. After these five minutes have been used, all your decisions are made by your DMs or habits. Its great if you have good DMs or habits. If you have bad DMs or habits, you are in deep trouble.

All your goal setting and planning becomes fatally flawed if only your DMs help you design them because you no longer have any choice in the matter. You are not exercising choice because you are in your DMs 99 percent of the time.

These are all examples of DMs:

- You get up in the morning, brush your teeth, and get ready for work
- You are chilling out with friends
- You get angry and frustrated when confronted by something outside your current skill sets
- When someone makes you angry and you experience amygdala hijack and storm away
- You make a business decision because you are angry with a competitor

Only when you understand this can you truly exercise choice in your default programs.

Your DM is your familiar prison. I will repeat this: the only choice you can meaningfully exercise is what DMs you invoke after you have made a decision. In other words, after you've decided / chosen, all your habits / DMs kick in. We live in a series of psychological prisons.

Key Questions:

What are your beliefs about success in life, health, and relationships?

Have you tested these beliefs?

What are your habits based on these beliefs?

Are your habits working for you or do you experience pain and discomfort?

Childhood Wounding

A great deal of time, in early childhood and young adulthood, is spent conforming. It is very traumatic to question one's true identity and, once it's discovered, to then feel it necessary to keep it secret from one's inner self, one's own family, and the outside world.

Early-childhood programming occurs as follows:

- We all begin life in a state of relaxed and joyful bliss.
- If our wants and needs are met, our state of relaxed and joyful bliss is sustained. Otherwise as our needs become increasingly unmet, negative programming begins.
- Our unmet need causes fear and pain. In our infantile ignorance, we have no idea how to change it and restore our feeling of safety. We adopt primitive coping mechanisms.

At the same time, throughout our childhood, we are also being programmed by our caretakers and communities to fit into society. We are programmed to do what we can to gain love and acceptance:

- We split off, repress or disown parts of ourselves that society finds challenging or unacceptable. Those of us with good enough caretakers get by; those who don't have their lives handicapped.
- We have the illusion that we have freedom of choice when it comes to choosing our life. However, our unconscious has an agenda of its own.
- Our primitive 'old' part of the brain has a compelling, non-negotiable drive and programming to restore us to the original blueprint.
- To restore us, the damage done in childhood because of unmet needs must be repaired. The way the unconscious does that is to design a life that would give us what our caretakers failed to provide.
- Every transaction of pleasure and pain in childhood has 'scarred' us, and we're always trying to replicate these transactions as we scan our environment for a suitable life partner. For example, if your mother was very controlling and you had to work very hard to get positive acknowledgement from her, you will be drawn to a partner who will replay your mother's role.
- This image of the "Internal Program" which can make me whole again I call the "Internalized Program".
- Consciously we may seek only the positive traits, but unconsciously the negative traits of our caretakers are in our "Internalized Program". These traits caused the painful experiences we now seek to heal. Our unconscious seeks to restore us by a program that reminds us of our caretakers. In other words, we look for circumstances that replicate the same deficits that hurt us in the first place.
- So when we fall in love, we do so with someone who is the sum total of all our caretaker characteristics. We end up in careers, life circumstances, that recreates the essence of our caretakers' lives.
- This guarantees more of the same pain and wounding that we experienced as children, until we learn to recognize this pattern and move into a more aware way of living. Otherwise you experience the hurts of your childhood all over again and wonder why love and life hurts.

- Why is it good to experience this conflict? Because the conflict makes us become aware, and we grow and make new choices.
- This is a natural-selection mechanism. Everything in nature is evolving by overcoming a challenge. This can be seen as conflict or emergence. Conflict that leads to higher levels of organization or emergence is a sign that the psyche is trying to survive, to get its needs met and become whole. It's only without this knowledge that conflict is destructive.
- Simply changing circumstances without emergence does not solve the problems. We may change our partners, jobs, houses, etc., but we keep our problems, carrying them forward into the next relationship, job, or house. We can solve the problem by undoing the fundamental negative childhood programs.

The Cave Allegory

In his book "The Republic", Plato, the famous Greek philosopher, has his teacher Socrates recount the allegory of the cave.

A group of people have lived since birth chained up in a deep cave, never ever seeing daylight, and are able to see only before them, but neither to the right nor to the left. Behind them is a fire. There is a low wall between the prisoners and the fire. There are various statues manipulated by a hidden group (representing all the forces that program and influence us) behind the low wall that the prisoners cannot see.

The prisoners see the shadows cast by the statutes on the opposite wall, the wall in front of them. The shadows are moving, and the prisoners think they are real. Most people mistake the products of their deletion, generalization, distortions, and projections as real and reflecting reality. They mistake their internal map of the world for the real world.

These prisoners represent people who have never asked questions about their lives. They have never realized their mental models were controlling them.

One of the prisoners is freed from his bonds and forced to confront the reality of the fire and statutes themselves. This is what happens when one day something shocking happens (you lose your job or someone close to you dies). You are shaken out of your trance state or default mode, wake up, and are forced to see the world as it is.

So the prisoner faces pain and confusion initially because his eyes are not used to the light. He then realizes that he is seeing the reality for the first time, as opposed to the shadows formed by the fire and the statues he previously saw.

He now accepts the fire and statues as most real. This stage in the cave represents belief. He is still unaware that there that there are things of greater reality — a world beyond his cave.

Like the prisoner, the first step to freedom is when you begin to wake up from your dream state and your default modes.

Next, this prisoner is dragged out of the cave into a world of sunlight. His eyes are blinded; initially he can look only at shadows, then at reflections. Finally, he can see what is real: trees, flowers, houses, and so on. He sees that these are even more real than the statues were, that the statues were only copies of these real objects. He has now reached the cognitive stage of thought. He has caught his first glimpse of the most real things, as they are.

When the prisoner's eyes have fully adjusted to the brightness, he lifts head and sees the sun. He understands that the sun is the root cause of everything around him — the light, his capacity for sight, the existence of flowers, trees, and other objects.

When you fully wake up from your dream state and your default modes and see the world for what it is, you become fully capable of choosing.

So the collective power of the DMs is that most people are not free to choose. So long as you buy into what the state, religion, and the financial system has to offer you, you are hooked. They in turn get a hardworking, docile member of their tribe working hard and paying his dues.

The state makes you pay taxes, religious organizations collect tithes and claim a monopoly on your soul, banks make 1,000 percent or more on what you save and pay you 1 percent or less. If you do so in full awareness of what is happening that is choice. If you do so because you do not know any other way, it is your default mode.

You can decide to enter a new relationship. Even how you enter it will be a function of default programs. Once it is status quo, you will default to old patterns. If those old patterns destroyed the previous relationship, they will destroy the new one.

So only true choice is that you can design and build new default programs/habits after you have awareness and clarity. Otherwise even if you hit all your goals and targets you are simply repeating the same old formula, even after you achieve all your goals there is a feeling of lack and inadequacy. This is the only way to have forward movement in your life. This is the secret that most programs do not address.

Everything I am about to share with you is the beginning of the exact process I followed to design the life of my dreams. And it's the plan that led me to experience less stress, more freedom, and more control over every aspect of my life.

More importantly, by following this process I have the comfort and the confidence of knowing I am always headed in the direction I want to go so I don't end up at a destination I didn't really choose. And that is what I want for you.

You wouldn't be watching this if you didn't want more in your life. That's why I want to make things straightforward and simple. So let's help you create a designed life starting with the first question. Ready?

The first question is: "What would your ideal life five years in the future look like?"

Most people life their lives as if they are going to live forever. There is this belief that there will be all the time to change. Life will carry on in pretty much the way it always has. There will be lots of time to adjust to the changes that will occur in their lives. At the right time pieces will just fall magically in place and it will all be as right as rain. They may not say it, but this is pretty much how they live it. They often give no thought to how the future will change and if they will be ready for it.

When I met Dan, who today is one of my business partners, he was an incredibly focused and driven person about his future while being very careful to maintain all his relationships with people. After he graduated as an engineer, he began working for an engineering company and decided he wanted to focus on being a management consultant.

After he completed his MBA, he tried to get a job. He figured he would have no problems with his double degrees and years of working experience. To his horror, he went through twenty-six interviews before he got a job. This gave him a foretaste of his probable future. When he finally got a job, he made a resolution that he would never be at the mercy of another interviewer.

Eventually he left, set up his own company, and began investing in other businesses. Fast forward five years. Today, he has invested in thirty companies in six countries in multiple industries. He got married to a very special lady who is studying to become a doctor, and now has a beautiful son. His major concern is how he can give his son a great life in the future.

What would your ideal future look like? What gets you excited and motivated about it?

The second question is:
"If you continued like you are doing now,
would you feel fulfilled five years in the future?"

Now one of the illusions of our culture is that you can do it all. And you know, I just don't buy it. I believe you can do anything you want, you just can't do everything you want, so if you are going to live a designed life it has to be based on priorities, i.e. intentionally choosing the priorities that'll guide your life.

Now you certainly know what's important to your husband or your wife. You probably know what is important to your boss. You may know what's important to your parents, or your kids. But who is setting the priorities of *your* life? What's important to you? Are you being honest with yourself?

Gabriel is a friend and client. We went to school together. Gabriel has attended my personal development programs. He consistently put other people in his life first. Gabriel had carefully worked out his financial plans so that when he retired he would have financial security six years in the future. When I met Gabriel's older brother, I felt disturbed. In my opinion, Gabriel and his brother had a serious co-dependent relationship.

Gabriel also had challenges with his ex-wife about getting access to his children. He later confided that he was backing his brother's businesses financially. I finally told Gabriel that he needed to do significant emotional work about his relationships with people. That it would take one year. If he chose not to do this, it would have serious repercussions on his future. I also mentioned that I would need to maintain strict neutrality and not hang out with him as a friend for that one year. Gabriel told me that it sounded too painful to do that type of work and he would prefer that we remained as friends.

Fast forward five years. Gabriel's brother defaulted on his loan, and the banks foreclosed on the loan. Since Gabriel was the guarantor of the loan, they went after him. In one year's time Gabriel would have achieved financial freedom for life. Instead at that point in time Gabriel was declared bankrupt. He then came in, too little, too late, to do emotional healing. Gabriel got very stressed. A latent heart problem got activated and became life threatening. He needed surgery to carry on. Fortunately, Gabriel survived the surgery.

If you continue like you are doing now, would you feel fulfilled five years in the future? Or do you need a rapid reality check on where you are going in your life?

Now here is the third question: "What commitment will you make now to your ideal future?"

Note on paper the various areas of life (e.g., family, financial, health, personal growth, professional, etc.) and rank them. Which is the most important area for you; which is the second most important, and so on.

This is a very helpful exercise because eventually one of the things that's going to happen particularly if you are a young parent is you'll have a choice to make. Are you going to attend that play with your daughter or are you going stay at the office and do that project your boss asked you to do at the last minute? What will be your guiding principle? What will be the priority that will influence you that moment?

If you are a planner like I am, and if you have any experience in the corporate world or with your own company, you know that business planning is everything. And I also believe in life planning. But there's this misconception when it comes to planning that you have to have it all figured out before you can take the first step.

Here is my dirty little secret: I rarely have it all figured out. I almost never see the end from the beginning. I usually know the next couple of steps, but I rarely know what steps I am going to take after that. Now a lot of people create really elaborate plans and that's fantastic if you are building a new hotel. But for most of us building an elaborate plan is just another way to procrastinate.

Now that you are clear about the questions you need to answer to live a life by design, the obvious next step is the practicality of implementing the answers on a daily basis. For example, how will your everyday life change from what you are currently doing? How will your daily decisions be different based on the answers to these questions? And how will you manage your time so that you are giving attention to the things that matter most? It's all just dreams and wishes unless we take our 30,000-foot view of our ideal life and bring it down to practical, daily actions.

This is critical because I'm sure you've wanted before to make a big change in some area of your life. But for some reason you didn't. Am I right? We've all been there, so what's going to be different for you this time? For most people, nothing. And that's the reason most people will never get what they truly want in life.

To succeed we've got to break these old habits. I had to. Being ultra-driven about my business, I needed a serious wake-up call to realize I had to do something dramatically different with the way I approached my day. If I didn't, I'd get sucked into the same old routine.

To make positive changes, to break a rhythm and routine that isn't serving us, we have to change. Now go ahead and answer the three questions above. I can't wait to see what new breakthroughs you will make.

Compulsive Life	Designed Life
I want to be a success	I want success on my terms
I don't need to manage my mental states	I must master the inner game to succeed
I don't have any negative mental programs	I need to rewrite limiting mental programs
If I work hard success will come my way	My top priority will decide how I succeed

Here are stories of those whose lives and goals changed after they had a break through.

A) EVALUATE

2) Identify the time and resources you have available.

https://youtu.be/MCFMQLMMaMg

4

ARE YOU MASTER OF YOUR DESTINY?

*A man who dares to waste one hour of time
has not discovered the value of life.*

Charles Darwin, **The Life & Letters of Charles Darwin**

If you have had thoughts about managing your life for greater productivity, be aware you can expect a challenging road ahead. If the path was painless, everyone would do it. Many of those who elect to manage their time for a fulfilling life end up not seeing it through.

Designing your life well has a tangible aspect to it. Any activity which you train for ahead of time will bring a greater outcome. You'll discover that the power of your mind will bring you towards your ambitions.

Regardless of how far back you bother to look, you will discover that individuals who are into Life Design had one major thing in common: they understood precisely what they were getting into. They knew precisely what Life Design for greater returns involved, they understood everything that was required of them to accomplish their main objective. When you understand precisely what it takes to manage your resources for greater productivity, there is no stopping you!

So what exactly do we know? Essentially, we know Life Design for greater productivity is not a painless task like having a typical life. Life

Design for better results requires that you be focused, relentless, and enlightened. Now that we understand this, we can move on to precisely what we need to do to make it happen.

You had previously asked yourself: "Do you want to do things faster?" This is the first step. People who answered "No" to this will be unable to make the first stride towards managing time for greater productivity.

You asked, "Do you want to achieve more with less effort?" You would not have gotten to this point if you had answered "No". The harsh reality is that while many people dream of managing their time for greater productivity, it takes a special type of individual to actually do it.

Congratulations for being that special type of person, the type that gets going. You are still reading this book.

Those who struggled to manage their time for greater productivity and failed probably did not adequately prepare. By reviewing the questions (Page 46) to establish if you are the right person to manage time for greater productivity, you now know what is essential to make it happen.

Always remember that building in buffer time for the unexpected will to ensure you will nearly always get things done. If you begin by keeping that in mind you can rise to the challenge.

Let's now move to priming yourself to remain focused on your essential priority, the one that will make a difference in your life.

The Internal Domino Effect

The 'internal domino' effect is a thought that pops up in your mind… that leads to another thought… and another… and all of a sudden, it's an hour later and you haven't gotten anything done. The internal domino effect can also be a single emotion that leads to another emotion, and another one… and all of a sudden you're worked up over nothing.

The internal domino effect can also begin with something physical, like losing your keys. As you're looking for them you find something else you haven't seen in a while, and that leads to something else... and you're totally distracted.

Multitasking can trigger your internal domino effect. In fact, many of us are "internal domino effect addicts". We get addicted to the stress chemicals that get released when we're distracted and stressed out chasing our dominoes around.

When you first notice your dominoes, it's a moment of "Being Present". It's becoming aware of what's been going on all along.

> **To do this, first write down a list of all the dominoes (or triggers) that distract you physically, emotionally, and mentally. Write down three-four in each area.**

Next, look at the list for the one BIGGEST domino. Then visualize yourself in a situation right when the domino shows up. See the scene begin to happen in super-slow motion.

Now, do the same visualization but this time see yourself "Being Present" just as the domino happens. You take a deep breath, let it go, and get back to what you were doing. And you feel good that you maintained your focus.

An Exercise That'll Help Us Get "Completion" On Things In Our Life

Parts of our life that are "incomplete" rob us of energy. Maybe you had a fight with someone years ago and you never really resolved it. Or someone ripped you off, and you have lingering resentment. Or you've been halfway done on a project for months.

> **First, make a list of all the areas of your life where you have a sense of "incompleteness." One page maximum at the most. It should take you less than ten minutes. Next, go through the list and prioritize the ones that are robbing you of the most energy. These are the ones we want to attack first. Either complete them, or let them go consciously.**

Decide it's just not worth it to allow them to rob you of energy any longer. This can be hard, because our ego can get involved. A lot of times, we'd rather "serve justice" on a person rather than get our life and energy back. Weird, I know. Instead, make the conscious decision to either get completion or "release it to the universe".

Most people can't sleep because they are obsessing about problems that are not theirs or problems they cannot solve. Very often they simply go around in circles because they have trained themselves to problem-solve without having a switch-off button.

Stressed and Overwhelmed

Stress cannot be eliminated by sleep or a bath. Often people under duress will not be able to identify or admit the precise reason for their stress, and start feeling the whole world is ganging up on them.

Pointing fingers, e.g. at vague and subjective issues, does not help you in finding solutions. How exactly do you pin point your stressors on your own?

There's a simple technique: ask yourself key questions to identify your stressors and manage them.

Stress Markers

The following questions will be a good way to identify stressors at work. This list should be enough to begin with; you can add more questions later.

- Do you have enough resources to do your job?
- Are the job specifications stated in measurable terms for what is expected of you?
- Do you have access to a Standard Operating Procedure (SOP) manual?
- Do you have to do everything yourself or do you have help?
- Are you trying to control issues outside your control?
- Are you trying to please or seek admiration from everyone?
- Are you an appreciation-seeking addict?
- Is somebody's urgency or poor planning an emergency for you?
- Is your life at the mercy of emails, pagers, other electronic-control mechanisms?
- Are the timeframes and work targets real?
- Are you chasing artificial deadlines created by clueless people?
- Are you burning out from chasing unrealistic expectations from everyone around?
- Are others expecting you to do mind reading and vice versa?
- Are you financially challenged? Are you spending more than you are earning?
- Is a corporate rumor about getting fired, downsizing, reorganization, etc., causing stress?
- Are you taking care of your health and rest properly?
- Are you getting your eight hours of calm sleep daily?
- Do you or your family have any known health problems that could trigger stress?
- Are family problems creating hell at work? Are work problems creating hell at home?
- Are you needlessly anticipating bad news?
- Are you working in a badly managed project?
- Having too little, too much or no work can create anxiety about job continuity
- Do you suck at time management? Are you overcommitted? Can you reduce your load?

The above list is a good way to start figuring out what is stressing you.

Stop Obsessing and Start Doing

Take out a piece of paper and write down all the things you obsess over, are worried about, think about, etc. Write for fifteen minutes straight. Do it now.

OK, done? That's a lot of stuff, isn't it?

Next, go through the list and put a check mark next to everything that is outside your control ("What I Cannot Control" list), and a star next to everything that is in your control ("What I Can Control" list).

Then take all the items with stars, pick the most important ones (no more than ten), transfer them to another list, and put them in descending order of priority. These are the things you are going to work on over the next eight weeks if you sign up for my online "Freedom Formula" program.

After you have prioritized the top ten items in your What I Can Control list, generate what you need to do to change the situation. You may find that as you generate solutions, there may be certain areas that you have no control over.

List changes you can make in the "What I Can Change" category. List issues that continue to come up under the "What I Cannot Change" category.

Consciously let go, in your mind, of whatever you have identified in the What I Cannot Control list and What I Cannot Change category. When you're done, you'll have released the things that are outside your control or not critically important, and you'll have a fresh new list of the most important things that you can control.

Every time you look at Life Design for greater productivity as a lifestyle (an ongoing process) instead of a goal, it becomes easier to adopt practices that augment your success. Adjustments in your schedule have a bigger purpose, one beyond realizing a single objective. The most dedicated people will see their main objective; you can become one of these people.

Take that first step. Allow yourself to become enlightened! You will find the journey a stimulating one.

Compulsive Life	Designed Life
I can control everything	I only focus on what I can control
I can change everything in my life	I only focus on what I can change
There are things that I cannot influence	I only focus on what I can influence
I am a spontaneous in how I plan	I have routines that help me win every time

If you need help developing a wellness program, check it out at:
www.sundardasnaturopathy.com

A) EVALUATE

3) Identify What Goals And Targets You Need To Achieve

https://youtu.be/N-01D7zSuxM

5

HAVE YOU LIVED WELL?

*"I wish it need not have happened in my time," said Frodo.
"So do I" said Gandalf, "and so do all who live to see
such times. But that is not for them to decide.
All we have to decide is what to do with the time that is given us."*

J.R.R. Tolkien, **The Fellowship of the Ring**

You need to be motivated to do Life Design. The rewards are enormous: a clear sense of direction, a fulfilling life, happiness. Remember, though, that everything you do must revolve around one major priority. Have more than one priority and eventually the clutter overwhelms you, and you get pulled in a thousand different directions.

Every time you are managing time for a fulfilling life, there are generally some critical actions you need to take. You certainly need to plan in three- or five-year chunks, plan backwards from three to five years to the present, and plan for tasks to be done in fifteen-minute chunks, i.e. tasks must be broken down into 15-minute chunks.

Regarding that last critical action: one of the most common reasons for procrastination is people don't know where to start. Only by ensuring a task has been broken down into its smallest possible chunks can a plan of action be executed.

These three actions don't merely help you out with good Life Design; more importantly, they bring forth other improvements in your life.

Life Design for a fulfilling life is something that has made many feel better about themselves.

Individuals who start planning in three- or five-year chunks recognize significant adjustments in their mental well-being. Those people feel better prepared to tackle other things in life.

Preparing ahead of time allows you to become stronger than you were before. This enables you to complete more than you could before, and not run out of energy as easily. More importantly, it helps to build up your mental and emotional "muscles" so that you are more resilient and capable when the situation calls for it.

Remember that you have classified yourself as a focused, relentless and enlightened kind of person. An enlightened self-starter is geared to manage time productively. He understands that unless he can break down each task into fifteen-minute chunks, he cannot plan to manage time for greater productivity.

80/20 Rule — Up Close & Personal

The 80/20 Rule or Pareto Principle is extremely important for growing any business. The Pareto Principle has been successfully applied to a variety of different areas and holds true in an astonishingly wide variety of fields. But it can have a down side as well as an upside.

Pareto Principle: The 80/20 Rule in Relationships

The Pareto Principle states that 20 percent of your activities likely contribute to 80 percent of your happiness. The Pareto Principle is perhaps most famous for its suggestion that successful people tend to achieve 80 percent of their results from only 20 percent of their activities. The 80/20 Rule is often used to improve productivity in people and businesses by identifying how time can be saved or used more effectively. Don't understand this principle and 80 percent of your effort will be expended to achieve just 20 percent of your results.

Small but Consistent Actions Over Time

Your time should be spent conducting business with your best clients. Efficiency should never be an end in itself, because when efficiency is made the goal, you are more often than not just making yourself busy rather than making yourself productive. Effective time managers will spend their time on the important objectives that help them attain their important goals. If you develop short-, medium-, and long-term goals, you can organize your time and tasks well.

Where you choose to work on your own productivity curve largely determines what you will accomplish in your work and your business. At the high end of the curve, the things you do have great value.

An Increasing Array of Marketing Messages

This principle is often referred to in business as you will get 80 percent of profits from just 20 percent of your clients. Some business experts go as far as suggesting you fire the 80 percent of unprofitable clients. By increasing sales to your best clients and businesses you can reduce your costs. By letting go of bad clients and focusing on selling and improving service to the best clients, your business will flourish.

For example:

Are you spending 80 percent of your productive time on activities that produce only 20 percent of your total results?

Or:

Are you spending 20 percent of your productive time on activities that produce 80 percent of your total results?

To help you discover which position you're in, let's do some research on your work habits and how you spend your productive time.

Over a three-day period, note how much time you spend on the following activities:

1) Business-related profit-producing
2) Business-related non-profit-producing
3) Personal activities

As you go through each day, jot down your activities and how long you spend on each activity. Be as accurate as you can. After you complete three days of activity tracking, go back and categorize your activities by business-related profit-producing, business-related non-profit-producing, and personal.

You can also include any categories you think are important and applicable to this exercise and your business. Make sure you make a note of the results you achieve from the time spent on each activity. Add up the time you spend on each category of activities over the three-day period. Add up the total time spent then calculate the percentage of the total that was spent on each category.

Now take a good look at what this exercise shows you:

- How did you spend your productive time? Was it on profitable activities or on non-profit-producing activities?
- What results were produced and what percentage of your productive time did it take to achieve these results?
- Was the total time spent on personal activities more than the time you spent on business activities?
- Was the time spent on non-profitable business activities more than the time you spent on profitable business activities?

If you're getting 20 percent of your results from 80 percent of your business activities, think about what needs to happen to turn the 80/20 Rule in your favor. It's all about knowing the value of your time and when your most productive time occurs. Then you can start leveraging your strengths to achieve your profitable activities before you spend time on anything else, especially non-profitable activities.

Form time-management habits that serve you well in the forty productive years (ages 25-65) you effectively have. The statistics are not encouraging. By 65:

- 1 percent are wealthy
- 4 percent are financially fit
- 5 percent are still working
- 28 percent are dead
- 62 percent are flat broke

So, let's roll up our sleeves and figure out together what the value of your time needs to be to get you where you want to be. Let's determine how you spent your time for three days. From that pattern, you will realize the following:

1) **Business-Related/Profit-Producing**
2) **Business-Related/Not-Profit-Producing**
3) **Personal**

You can maximize your dollar value per hour only by increasing #1.

What Is An Hour Of Your Time Worth?

I don't mean to get all philosophical on you, but have you ever really thought about your time?

If you really think about it, time is all you have. Time is life. Moreover, there's no such thing as free time. You can't save free time and use it later. You have leisure time but it's not free time.

You are either using your time purposefully or wasting it. Leisure time is time that you use for rest and creation. You have *chosen* to spend your time this way — it is not by default.

What does this mean for your business or your life? Unless you commit to continually increase the value of your time, you will not be making the kind of money in your business you want or working the fewer number of hours you want.

There is no free time. You pay for all your time with your life. If you don't use it, you lose it and all its effects: your income level, your health, and your relationships. In short, if you don't value your time, no one else will.

It always intrigues me that people generally have no idea what their time is worth and how to increase its value. So the question is, "What is your time worth?" Do you know what your time is worth? Do you know how to value your time to achieve your income goals?

Unless you know the value of your time, your capability to make effective decisions on what you should or shouldn't be doing, whether you should be delegating, is fatally compromised.

This exercise challenges your perception of the value of time. If you're honest — and I hope for your sake you are — you get tremendous clarity about why you are or are not be making the kind of progress you want. You and I both know it's easy to fall onto the trap of 'everyday life'.

Every year that passes is another year that we can end up drifting further and further away from the life we truly want. The seeds of doubt start creeping in. We think: *maybe I was never meant to be a writer, maybe she never really loved me, or maybe I'll never be able to lose this weight.* Deep down we know what we're capable of, but the idea of reaching that potential becomes a steeper and steeper hill to climb.

Here's a reality check: you *can* have your best year ever. But if we want to achieve progress towards the things that really matter, then we have to change our approach, we have to get clear about how our big goals translate into day-to-day actions.

And today, we're going to take the first step with a specific set of simple actions. So, whatever you like to accomplish in your career, relationships, or health, or whatever the impact you want to have in your community and the world, this tool will give you what you need to know, what it takes to stay on track so that life doesn't lead you astray. That's why this section is designed to help us get intentional.

If we're going to make this next year our best year ever, we've got to be intentional. The exercise I'm going to walk you through is designed to take a 30,000-foot view of your ideal life and bring that vision down to the daily actions you need to get there. More importantly, it's going to help you identify where to spend your time so that months or years don't pass before you take any action towards the things that matter most.

If you're someone who's coasting along, this exercise will ensure that you'll stay on track over the next twelve months. This exercise will bring intention into everything you do. And if you're the type of person who's been living a compulsive life, one where you've been very focused on achieving results in just one or two areas of your life at the expense of the other areas, then this exercise will help you channel your ambition and ensure that you win at work AND succeed at life.

Before I explain how this exercise works, let me clarify why I developed it. Anyone who knows me, reads my blog, or attends my programs knows I've always been a high achiever.

As a physician, professor, and award-winning entrepreneur and best-selling author, I've always had really big goals. And for a long time, I was very focused on my career. The outside world was doing well. The problem was that I achieved these big goals at the expense of my family and health.

Finally, I realized that everything that really mattered to me was suffering. I understood that the wins were not worth the trade-offs; I knew something had to change. This was true not only for my personal life but also for my professional life.

Now my mission is to help people both win at work and succeed at life. What I missed for years is that these goals are only achieved in tandem. If we're doing one at the expense of the other we eventually fail at both. So I got intentional.

I started really thinking about the big picture. What would my future life look like? What was the change I was committed to making?

I got clear about what was important to me. I committed to making the things that mattered a real priority. Then I started to get practical: I looked for ways to make daily progress towards my big goals. I knew the drill; I had had aspirations before this, but nothing changed because my habits didn't change. So this time I committed to breaking the cycle.

Through a process of discovery, I developed this exercise. Now every year this has become the very first step I take in setting my goals. In fact, this eventually became the foundation of my expanded "Freedom Formula — Mastering Energy, Money, and Leverage in 9 Steps" online program. This process has now helped many of my clients live a life by design and achieve much more.

Now I'm going to give you more of the building blocks. Let's start with one simple exercise. It's going to open your eyes to what's really going on — the good, the bad, and yes, the ugly — with your time. No more going into default mode and hoping success just comes to you. Today, we're getting intentional. We're taking the first step towards designing life the way we want it. Are you ready? Let's get started.

We've all heard that time is money. The problem is that we don't actually act like it's true… but what if we did? That's exactly what my "What Is Your Time Worth?" exercise does for you.

Here's the reality: right now you have some big decisions about what you're going to do with your time. Maybe there are some enticing opportunities on the horizon you feel like seizing, but that you wouldn't take if you knew the cost. Or maybe you have a project or a business you need to exit to make room for something better. But the only way you'll know is if you can determine the real dollar value of your available time.

We drift usually because we're not intentional. We mindlessly keep adding opportunities and projects to our schedules, and our lives are filled with mindless, never-ending lists of things to do till one day our heart ceases. NOW we've got a crisis on our hands, and who's got time for that?

The best way to determine the real value of your available time is to work backwards from how much revenue you're currently making. Next, notice the five big blocks: Time off, Time on, Administration, Service Delivery and Revenue Generation. We have only 365 days in a year (366 if it's a leap year); how we divide those days is critical for understanding how much they're worth. Take the total amount of revenue (or income) we're projecting and divide it by the days we have available to earn it. Right away we want to subtract the number of days we're taking off. This is your actual time available.

Current Value of Time

Total Current Revenue / Total Number of Days = Dollar Value Per Day (eight-hour day formula)

This tells you how much you are really making a day.

Next, best way to do that is to work from how much revenue you're going to be earning.

Projected Value of Time

Total Projected Revenue / Total Number of Days = Dollar Value Per Day (eight-hour day formula)

If you are an entrepreneur, business owner, or CEO, this exercise is for you. Practice working on profit building for an hour. At first it won't be easy. Eventually you will be able to go the distance; you'll spend a solid hour on profit-building activities. That is what productive time is all about. Productive time is time directly related to generating income. So what percentage of the time are you productive?

The above exercise shows you your dollar value per day. However, what will really get to you is: how much of your day is actually productive?

Right now, I'm taking ninety-nine days off each year. 365-99 gives me 266, the days I have left for work. I take this figure of 266 and break it up into three, as follows.

Remember the exercise on Page 66 where you listed all the activities you performed over a three-day work period? Well, I did the same: I sat down and tracked for three days how I spent my working time, noting everything I did. I looked at time spent on:

1) **Administration**
2) **Service Delivery**
3) **Revenue Generation**

Administration refers more to maintenance stuff: running meetings, answering email, returning calls, and so on. This is the time I'm working on the business. Look at it this way: there are things you need to do to maintain your business, and there are things you need to do to grow your business. Here's a pro tip: the better you can manage to have separate days for the activities of each category, the more focus and efficiency you'll build.

Service Delivery is when I am doing medical-related activities or I am teaching a program and there is no selling involved.

Revenue Generation for me is activities such as creating video courses, blogging, writing books, conducting seminars, selling to clients, etc. For you it could be the different businesses in your portfolio, the different customers your accounts will serve, it could be creating a product, making sales calls, and whatever turns the crank in your business.

Figure out how many days you have to generate revenue; these become your Revenue Generation Days. Take your Total Revenue Target and divide by your Revenue Generation Days to compute how much those days are really worth.

Every day you're working just to maintain the business, not creating revenue, you're potentially wasting time. I encourage you to think about re-doing this exercise several times over the next few days.

I was shocked to realize that I was spending only fifteen percent of my time on revenue-generating activities, so I decided to change how I spent this time. I started delegating more of the Administration and Service Delivery activities to others, and began to focus more on Revenue Generation.

Doing this exercise gets very sobering, very fast. But it's also empowering. When I first did this exercise, I found I was spending a great deal of time on activities that were not generating revenue. It took me a while to make the decision, but I eventually decided to reconfigure how I ran some of my businesses.

You'll notice the first critical piece of information: how much money are you projecting to make this coming year? We want to put dollar signs on our days so we can see how much our time is worth. I think you'll be surprised at the figures you see.

What are your results telling you? Whatever the answer, doesn't it feel empowering knowing where you should be spending your time? Clarity is a wonderful thing — even if it's depressing news at first.

The first time I went through this exercise, I was shocked. I couldn't believe the deficit I was experiencing, but it explained a lot. Immediately

I could see why work was creeping into my weekends and into my nights. And from that, it was easy to see how I was not maximizing the limited time I had for the important things in life.

Productive time is time directly generated to income. So what percentage of the time are you productive? One study of Fortune 500 CEOs estimated they had twenty-eight productive minutes a day. Another one estimated it at thirty-eight productive minutes a day. Shocking figures, wherever between them the actual number of productive minutes a day lies? (But think about what a CEO does. Can you do any better?) However most of us are not working at that level so we can afford to be a lot more productive.

Compulsive Life	Designed Life
There are many things I do well	There is only one thing I am brilliant at
I will go after every opportunity	I will focus only on my core competence
There are many things I can do to impact the bottom line right now	There is only priority I need to focus on to increase the bottom line

https://youtu.be/adf482a0WCo

6

ARE YOU SPENDING YOUR TIME PROFITABLY?

There is only one success — to be able to
spend your life in your own way.

Christopher Morley

This chapter is aimed primarily at CEOs, entrepreneurs, and people in sales and marketing, though other people will find it interesting. Those in the first three roles will find this chapter crucial to their physical, emotional, and mental wellbeing and their time management.

This chapter examines attitudes about money and your profile or identity around time and money. "Know Thyself" is even more important when it comes to time and money management. This chapter summarizes research that has been conducted by the author around the psychology of achievement and time management.

How We Think About Money

I am sure everyone, at least once in his lifetime, has wondered how important money is to him. Money is an important part of life and affects us in all areas of our lives either directly or indirectly. What are the underlying reasons for your emotions about money?

Our attitude towards money affects all our choices be they in relationships, careers, or education. What thoughts come to mind when you think about money? How do you feel about and use money? Why do you even have that attitude? Do you know the difference between wealth and money?

The Difference Between Wealth And Money

Those who consistently build wealth-making machines understand the difference between wealth and money. If you know only how to make money, when you lose your money you cannot generate it again. If you know the difference between wealth and money, and you lose all your money, you can still generate wealth and make money.

There are different levels of education when it comes to wealth. Each level of education brings more and more wealth:

1. Get a job without much education and get a minimum wage like working in a fast-food joint.
2. Get a diploma or degree and your salary will be triple that.
3. Work in the area where you got your diploma or degree and you have higher prospects for advancement.
4. Become educated about wealth creation and you can begin the road to creating your own wealth mechanisms.

Are you on Level 1, 2, 3 or 4?

Also, there are three levels of awareness on the pathway to creating wealth:

1. Get a good education and work for someone or a company. You will then get a salary and live from pay check to pay check, hoping you touch the lottery or get an inheritance. Research has shown that no one to date who won a lottery has remained rich.
2. Start your own business and start managing the lives of other people who work for you. Learn all about cash flow, return on investment, and how to market your products and services.

3. Begin a journey on the path to becoming a Wealth Creator. At this level, you understand your innate wealth-creation pathways. You are also aligned with your values and beliefs and have the necessary habits to perpetuate your mechanisms of wealth.

Where are you on the above three levels?

We live at a time of tremendous possibilities in Asia. While opportunities abound, less than five percent of the general population will become self-made millionaires. What distinguishes this successful group from the rest is that they understand there are certain rules about creating wealth.

They understand the difference between money and wealth. They also understand the importance of being educated about wealth. To become a wealth creator you need to understand your 'Wealth Creation Blueprint'. This Blueprint, which is about being truly healthy, wealthy, and wise, consists of the following components:

1) **Your core values and beliefs about making money (Personal Success Blueprint)**
2) **Your innate psychological type. This is the type that determines what is the best pathway for you to build your money-creation machine (Profit Profile)**
3) **An overview of your habits and whether they support you in making money. Your 10,000-hour expertise (ages thirteen to twenty-one)**

Later we shall look at the core qualities of the Wealth Creation Blueprint. Click on the link at the end of the chapter to do a test.

1) Personal Success Blueprint

We all have a blueprint that decides how we handle our life. It's deeply ingrained in our subconscious and unconscious; it determines your life destiny. It comes from 'past programming', things we were conditioned or programmed by in childhood.

A few days after I got my first doctorate (more than twenty-three years ago), I woke up in the middle of the night screaming in panic, thinking to myself, "I need to get another doctorate!" That was the point when I realized I had a very deep emotional program that was limiting me. Over the next few days, I self-hypnotized myself and went back to the key incident in my past when this programming had occurred.

I had a very difficult time being born; indeed, I had almost died. I had 'decided' as a newborn that I could live only if I worked hard and did outstanding things.

That day, at thirty-one years of age, I changed this pattern. That year my relationship with my wife changed positively and my clinic income grew by 40 percent, even though I did nothing different.

Many people struggling with relationship issues may be unaware that the challenges they are facing are rooted in their early childhood, that they have acquired programming that interferes fatally with a happy love life. As a result of dysfunctional patterns in early childhood, they may build up inappropriate models of relationship on an unconscious level.

So while consciously they want a happy love life, on an unconscious level they are re-enacting an early childhood pattern.

You can be programmed for spending or saving in childhood. Some do both in cycles that keep them financially treading water their whole lives. There are those who instinctively choose winning investments and those who consistently pick losers. But how do you know which way your blueprint is set?

One Way Is To Look At Your Results!

Financial settings are like the temperature in a room. If the thermostat is set for 68 degrees, the room temperature is 68 degrees. If you are not earning enough, keeping enough, or enjoying your money enough, then your blueprint is set for "not enough". Your current financial blueprint will stay with you for the rest of your life, unless you change it.

One of the main objectives of the Personal Success Blueprint is to show you:

- How your childhood conditioning is affecting your life today
- How to identify and change your personal health, wealth, relationship, and success blueprints forever
- How to use 'spiritual laws' to create 'real-world' success
- How successful people think, and how to adopt their ingrained blueprint for abundance
- How to recondition your mind for 'automatic' success
- Whether you are attracting or repelling success.

Another thing you will learn is that the universe is dynamic. Everything is in a constant state of motion and change. You are either attracting success or repelling it, depending on how you think, speak, and act in the world.

At the Wealth Creation Blueprint Seminar, through intense reconditioning exercises, you will change your blueprint, resetting it for automatic success. Once you have done that, you will find that you will attract all that you have been struggling to achieve.

The Wealth Creation Blueprint Seminar objective is to help you achieve success in all areas of your life — your natural way of being!

By the end of the program, you will have a completely different unconscious attitude towards health, wealth, relationship, and success. If you choose to use the information, you will develop a winner's mind-set. You can create inner peace and happiness by using the same principles you learn to enhance your financial life. The Wealth Creation Blueprint Program (the two-day seminar, the book, and the manual) will teach you to be rich in every sense of the word.

Family of Origin Issues

Many people do not quite understand how 'family-of-origin' issues affect them.

Family-of-origin issues may include such issues as having grown up in alcoholic or chemically-dependent family systems, witnessing domestic violence, having lost a parent early through death, having an absent parent, being adopted, being a child of divorced parents or having had step-family issues, being a survivor of childhood neglect or emotional/physical/sexual abuse, having a parent who raged or was a workaholic, growing up in a family system plagued with eating disorders, having had a mentally-ill parent or a sex-addicted parent, or having been brought up with a strict religious orientation that somehow was causing conflict for the person in adulthood.

All these and numerous other situations can chronically change your set-point for health, wealth, and happiness. Addressing family-of-origin issues is not about placing blame but rather about healing unresolved trauma, and increasing awareness and gaining new perspectives about dysfunctional patterns that clients re-enact in adulthood.

If you have negative programs in your unconscious then you need to clear these programs. Once you do this, your world view and your mind set changes dramatically. Than whatever you set your mind to can be easily achieved.

When we work with individuals on deep-seated issues, they experience significant changes within twenty-one days of the process. Within twenty-one days, they make more money, their relationships change, or their health issues begin to significantly change, depending on the issue that was worked on.

2) Profit Profile

There are nine major Profit Profiles with three variations each. This profile will provide you with:

1. Clarity on the nine paths of least resistance to success
2. Identifiable role models and biographies within each path
3. A process for building the right team and focusing on the right activity
4. The growth stage of a business, and the members of the team you need, it matches
5. The essential hierarchy of your life values from passion to purpose.

Where Will This New Knowledge Lead You?

You find that wealth is far more about focus than talent, and that much of your time is focused on the wrong thing. When you quit focusing on these areas, you begin to experience entirely different levels of action, traction, and attraction. You find that there are rules to wealth and that until you begin to follow these rules, you'll never win the game. When you learn the rules, you realize you have the power to master them.

You realize the game that you need to play is already built around your strengths and passions — things you are likely to have been taking for granted while you work for a living. You begin to experience 'flow', which occurs when you follow your natural path. You begin to attract the right opportunities, people, talent, and resources.

You begin to master the art of anticipation, which can come only as a result of following your natural game. You discover that synchronicity, coincidences, and sheer luck are experiences that should not be left to chance. You find that as you increase your power to receive, you increase your power to give. You realize that your power to contribute becomes more than a choice: it becomes a responsibility. Momentum brings meaning, and your life path leads to your life purpose.

3) Your 10,000 Hour Expertise (Ages 13 to 18)

In *Outliers*, Malcolm Gladwell focuses on outliers, defined by Gladwell as people who do not fit into our understanding of normal achievement. Outliers are exceptional people, especially those who are smart, rich, and successful, and those who operate at the extreme outer edge of what is statistically possible. For example, Malcolm Gladwell interviews Bill Gates and outlines the opportunities given to him throughout his lifetime that led to his success.

A common theme that appears throughout *Outliers* is the "10,000-Hour Rule", based on a study by Anders Ericsson. The 10,000-Hour Rule states that it takes 10,000 hours to develop expertise in a craft such as music, writing, art or dance. If you become clearer about what you focused on from the ages of thirteen to eighteen — during which period you are likely to have completed your 10,000 hours — you will become clearer about where to focus your wealth-creation efforts.

Once you understand your Profit Profile, you can make sure that you live a life that is aligned with your core competence and your personalized Wealth Blueprint.

Compulsive Life	Designed Life
I can do it by willpower alone	I can win by focusing on my Profit Profile
I can work hard and make money	I can build systems to create wealth
It's all about me	It's about systems, my team, and me being aligned

B) DISCARD

Discard The Irrelevant

Refer to the shoe metaphor we started off with in chapter 1 (page 26). You have become really clear about what matters. You know what shoes you must keep, what you should sell, and what you should throw. However, are you really ready to get rid of what you should "throw away"?

In other words, it is not enough to identify what activities and commitments do not work for you. You have to actively discard them. Part Three of this book will show you how to discard the "clutter" in your life so that you can have a well-designed and meaningful life and make vital contributions in what really matters. You will also do it in such a way that you become more respected, acknowledged, and valued in your home, workplace, community, and society at large.

Getting rid of the shoes will not be easy. There will be that nagging fear that you gave away the specially-designed shoes that would have been perfect for the awards ceremony you have been invited to. This feeling is perfectly normal. Research has shown that when we don't own something we value it less. Those that we own we assign a higher value to and so find it harder to dispose of. The critical question is, "If I did not own this shoe, how much would I be prepared to spend to buy it?" Similarly, the critical question when deciding what to declutter is, "If I did not have this opportunity, what would I be prepared to sacrifice to get access to it?"

Of course, throwing away old shoes is a lot easier than saying "No" to what seems like an incredible opportunity coming your way. However, remember that in the Life Design model, whenever you don't say "No" to something, you are agreeing by default.

It's easier to become clear by asking yourself, "Instead of saying 'Yes' to every opportunity and activity, what would I say 'No' to?" This question will clear the cobwebs and give you great clarity for you and your team. It is the core questions that will allow you to make breakthroughs in your life, your career, and your business.

B) DISCARD

4) Identify What Is Irrelevant, Intrusive, And Drains Energy

https://youtu.be/rKol1TMiwqM

7

ARE YOU READY FOR CHANGE?

You can have it all. Just not all at once.

Oprah Winfrey

The following are stages that people go through on the journey of change:

1. Pre-contemplation
2. Contemplation
3. Preparation
4. Action
5. Maintenance
6. Relapse

It is important to understand when approaching an intervention or change that one size does not fit all. You go through different stages; being aware of the "Stages of Model Change" (by researchers James O. Prochaska, John C Norcross and Carlo C. Diclement), and appreciating that there is a specific transition at every point, makes the journey more manageable.

It's important to recognize that your aspirations are personally worthwhile and meaningful. You also need to practice patience: it takes a while to let go of old behavior patterns. It often takes twenty-one to thirty days of resisting the temptation and staying on track before new habits become second nature to you.

You should look at your positive gains and give yourself credit for what you have accomplished as you go through the roller coaster of change.

Finally, a normal part of making changes in your behavior is that you occasionally may attain one stage only to regress to a previous stage.

Stages to Change

Pre-Contemplation Stage
No consideration of change
In denial (it doesn't apply to me)
Feelings of 'immunity' (things happen to other people; consequences are not serious)
Given up (tried unsuccessfully in the past; believe there is no control)
Getting the client to think about change

Contemplation Stage
Undecided about change
Views change as a loss despite possible gain
Recognizes need for change but evaluates barriers ("yes, but… time, expense, hassle", etc.)
May spend some time considering options
May have to recognize barriers to change and benefits of making change
Getting through the contemplation stage may take anything from a few weeks to a lifetime.

Preparation Stage
There is a commitment to change
Prepares for or experiments with small change
May make a 'sample' change, e.g. in dietary or exercise recommendations, or decreasing bad habits

Action Stage
Takes definitive action to change
This is the shortest of all the stages. It can take from an hour to six months

Maintenance

Maintains behavioral change long term
May need to constantly reformulate the rules of life and acquire new skills in order to avoid a relapse

Relapse

Those who fail to adequately prepare often relapse later
They are unprepared for the trials and tribulations of change
The hastier the decision the higher the chances of relapse
May need support with maintaining the change
May need encouragement through admiration and praise

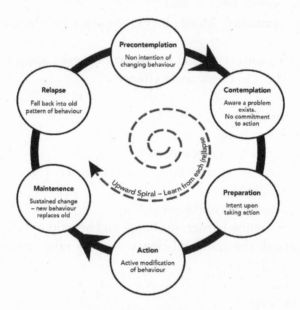

Fig: Stages of Change

Stages of Learning

There are five stages of learning:

Unconscious Incompetence:

Don't know that I don't know. Don't care to know. There may be a belief that the subject matter is too trivial or not important enough to warrant time and energy. "It's so easy any idiot can do it."

Conscious Incompetence:

Increasing awareness of ignorance. Increasing awareness of potential benefits of wanting to know more about the subject matter and learn some of the skills involved. This is an essential stage necessary to trigger the next stage of learning. "How does anyone ever learn this?"

Conscious Competence:

Conscious awareness of theory, framework, skill sets, and ability to use.

Using all of the above in problem solving. This is the beginning of expertise. "I can do this."

Unconscious Competence:

This is the stage where observation, theory, analysis, perspective, and discovering a solution are so seamless and automatic that it seems to flow and meld together. The answer seems so obvious that it seems hard to believe no one else can see it. "It is so obvious. How come no one else sees this?" This is the domain of an expert or the level of a habit.

Reflective Competence:

In order to reach the stage of reflective competence, the master requires a "beginner's mind", which refers to having an attitude of openness, eagerness, and lack of preconceptions when studying a subject, even when studying at an advanced level, just as a beginner in that subject would.

"In the beginner's mind there are many possibilities, but in the expert's, there are few."

When deliberately assuming the attitude of the beginner's mind, the master will reflect on the field of study and attempt to break every concept down to its simplest form. Attempting to do this will be counter-productive at earlier stages — it will interfere with the process of developing superior, automated, skill sets. Only when the superior skill sets are automated will the inquiry into first principles be useful.

Only when you instruct enough will you build up a sample base sufficient to identify patterns of development and progress. Only when you can accurately assess an individual's progress and specific skill attainments can you help them achieve the next level of development and growth.

In this schema, you have reached the grand master stage when you can do the following. As soon as you meet someone for the first time you are able to identify their current stage of development. You also know what it would take for them to move to the next level of attainment.

I have reviewed my personal diaries that I started when I was fourteen years old. They review my life from ages four to about early fifties. So I have had the opportunity to measure how only when I had new default programs in place (that were built over twenty-one days) did I truly exercise choice.

My time with my wife and time for my own health and fitness was crucial for building my tanks. When those things got out of balance, it impacted everything else. We'll all want to do well in our work life, I get it. But you can't compromise your commitment to self-care or the relationships that matter most; the tradeoff is never worth it. If we try doing one at the expense of the other we eventually fail at both.

Every new project that I initiated was conceptualized ten to twenty years ago. There was nothing inherently new. It's simply because I have noted this. I have observed this is true for all my clients as well. This means that for the rest of the book consider the following questions:

KEY QUESTIONS

1) **What areas of your life do you want to simplify and make new choices in?**
2) **What do you have to give up to become more efficient?**
3) **What are you prepared to omit to build relevant default programs/habits? (Note: every default program must be chunked down to fifteen minutes or less. A detailed program on how to do this is my online "Freedom Formula: Mastering Energy, Money, and Leverage in 9 Steps")**
4) **What do you have to cut out to have sufficient resources to design what you want?**
5) **What type of schedule would you have to design?**
6) **How would you execute it?**

So when you get clear like this, it can be incredibly empowering. And clarity will build momentum; momentum encourages confidence; and the clarity and confidence aligns your subconscious mind to start working for you rather than against you. The new big thing in this world: you need to protect your confidence. You have to equip yourself with every possible advantage.

This exercise will jump start that process for you. But ask yourself this as you move forward: "How will I maintain momentum throughout the entire year?" How will I build on that foundation that I've said here today? We've all been excited for short bursts of time, haven't we? But you've come this far so I know you're not someone who's interested in short bursts of success. We're playing the long game, right?

We want a life that continually gets better and better every week, every month, and every year. We want to look back twelve months from now with a deep sense of satisfaction, knowing that we've just had the best year of our lives. That means we have to put things in place that build on the momentum of today. We have to break our old habits and safeguard our success. Does all this make sense? Read on.

Compulsive Life	Designed Life
I can achieve by willpower alone	I need regular routines to hit my targets
I jump into new things easily	I design routines that make it possible to achieve

B) DISCARD

5) Eliminate Habits And Behaviors And Commitments That Do Not Serve You

https://youtu.be/6Y61L2EyBeA

8

ARE YOU IN THE NOW?

How did it get so late so soon?

Dr. Seuss

In **The Power of Full Engagement,** Tony Schwartz talks about the idea that most of us, most of the time, mix together different things we're doing. We rarely focus on just one thing at a time, and this robs us of both enjoyment and productivity. This is related to Neural Dissonance.

In the past several years, the latest brain-scan technologies have revealed that it's your pain and fear circuits that keep you from achieving your best. These new insights also reveal how to overcome and replace the limiting habits and beliefs that keep you stuck at your current success and income level.

Here are the facts: your brain is split into **three parts**. The reptilian (oldest) part of your brain keeps you away from anything that is (or is even *imagined to be*) threatening. Your rational, logical mind (neocortex) analyzes the ideas and plans that make it past your initial fear/comfort barriers.

But it's your emotional (limbic) brain that is the actual decision maker when it comes to whether or not you will *take the decisive action* that will determine whether you achieve your goals and dreams.

The average person gets one interruption every eight minutes — approximately seven an hour or fifty-sixty per day. The average interruption takes five minutes, totaling about four hours or 50 percent of the average workday. 80 percent of those interruptions are typically rated as "little value" or "no value" creating approximately three hours of wasted time per day.

Here's why knowing the above facts about your brain is crucial to the future you envision for yourself and even for planning for the future.

Your emotional desires, beliefs and values must align for you to be productive. When they don't align with the rational (logical) and instinctual (reptilian) brain and the emotional (limbic) brain, the three parts of your brain will constantly be fighting each other. This will mean your ability to succeed at anything, especially your goals to grow and support yourself and your family, will be fatally flawed.

This mental tension is called "Neural Dissonance". It's like having one foot on the accelerator while the other is on the brake, every day. You make some progress, then sabotage it. Over and over again. Day after day. It gets very tiring, doesn't it?

If you're tired of struggling to break through, the #1 thing to do right away is to create "Neural Coherence" where your logical, instinctual and emotional parts of the brain working are in a state of harmony.

Let's say you have a great family, and you also have great work that you do. And let's say the work is intense, and you've become a workaholic. When you're at work, you're thinking about how you should be spending more time with your family. When you're with your family, you're thinking about work.

In this chapter, we'll discuss the most common distractions we face at work, and we'll look at strategies for minimizing or eliminating them.

In this book, I adopt the stand that being under stress is a prerequisite for a high-quality physical, mental and emotional life.

How many of these common illusions about stress do you buy into?

- Stress is evil and should be avoided
- If you avoid stress you will be happy
- Being under stress makes you ill
- Your productivity and efficiency in life is related to you minimizing stress in your life
- As you age your capacity to weather stress goes down
- Your brain and body are gradually worn away by stress
- When many negative things happen to you, you are under stress

---

Standard Stress Management Programs

Conventional thinking about stress revolves around the following ideas:

- In order to manage stress, you must absolutely avoid all forms of stress in your life. So those who accept this perspective will identify all stressful areas in their lives. Many of them may even give up their jobs and drop out of society, saying it is too stressful
- The other perspective is that you need to stress-proof your life so that you become tough and strong. These people belong to the school of becoming harder, stronger and fitter. They often do such a good job of this that they start resembling battle tanks rather than people. Eventually one of the tubes or pipes (normally the major blood vessels to the heart) becomes "corroded" in such individuals and they fall apart or drop down dead.

The critical issue in this question about stress is the difference between stress exposure and stress response. Stress exposure is a powerful incentive for growth and development. We all develop in the areas in which we have experienced the most stress exposure, provided that as we exercise these "muscles" in response to stress we also rest and recuperate. Then these physical, mental and emotional "reflexes" continue to become stronger with time.

What makes many a person fall apart is their stress response. The constant stress of meeting quotas, losing business deals, facing unreasonable bosses, and dealing with incompetent employees, not to mention operating in an unfavorable economy, is not what tears you apart. It is your response to these issues that determines what happens next. Many people begin the spiral towards poor coping mechanisms and ill health because of their inappropriate emotional response.

The main thrust of this book revolves around creating balance amongst the different components of life and developing a range of specific strategies for a variety of situations.

What Is Stress?

Remember the last time you were under extreme stress? Since this could involve any demand or pressure that induced mental and physical tension, any incident could come to mind.

Stress can result from something happening around us or from something happening within. This can be a family crisis, a work problem, or a personal crisis. The primary effect of stress is to mobilize the body's "fight, flight or fright" system. This means that stress stimulates the chemical, physical, and psychological changes that prepare us to cope — via fight, flight or fright — with a threatening situation.

This may be appropriate when the stressful situation demands action. In fact, we can even speculate that such a system evolved back when the 'fight' impulse, was directed towards defending one's territory or competing for a mate; when flight meant running for one's life from a wild animal; and when 'fright' referred to confrontation with a natural disaster.

Being promoted, for example, stresses the body in much the same way as not being promoted. Both produce what Hans Selye, MD (the father of Modern Stress Medicine) called the General Adaptation Syndrome: a bodily reaction to stressful situations that involves emergency activation of both the nervous system and the endocrine (hormonal) system.

If you were to type the word 'stress' in any internet search engine you will get a billion pieces of information related to stress and the harm it can cause. A general dictionary defines stress as:

"A specific response by the body to a stimulus, as fear or pain that disturbs or interferes with the normal physiological equilibrium of an organism; mental or emotional strain or tension."

Daily, millions of people around the world experience stress ranging from mild to extreme cases that lead to several health disorders. According to Dr. Hans Selye, headaches, insomnia, high blood pressure, and heart and kidney diseases can be triggered by stress. He states, *"Every stress leaves an indelible scar, and the organism pays for its survival after a stressful situation by becoming a little older."*

Your adrenal glands produce a hormone called *cortisol* when stressed. Cortisol is a highly toxic substance that attacks muscles and organs, and rapidly diminishes your strength.

Cortisol also weakens your immune system leading to various kinds of mental and physical disorders. Stress is your body's natural response to every day's physical, emotional, and environmental stressors.

The immediate action of the nervous system and the time-release action of the endocrine system is to prepare and maintain the body for life-saving action. If stress is short term there is no problem since the body will have time to rest afterward.

Long-term stress, however, produces a progression of side effects. The General Adaptation Syndrome, for example, shifts blood flow to large skeletal muscles and decreases flow to the gastrointestinal tract and the skin. The first signs of such shifts might be cold hands and feet, then gradually a pale or shallow complexion, and finally migraine headaches or high blood pressure. There is an enormous amount of research to suggest that most major illnesses like heart conditions and high blood pressure are due to unresolved and/or unmanageable stress.

Stress per say is not bad. Indeed, we can argue that all the advances of human civilization occurred because of a variety of stress factors. What is important is that executives need to train and condition themselves to stress. It is exposure to higher levels of stress than they are prepared to handle that leads to catastrophe.

As we become conditioned to higher levels of stress, like the battle-seasoned warrior, every potentially stressful occasion becomes an opportunity to rise to the challenge. Conversely, all the clients I saw had been pushed beyond their ability to cope and were experiencing illness, breakdown, and demoralization as a result. Some psychosomatic effects of 'bad' stress can be very difficult to manage.

The two major polar responses to stress are as follows:

- If you are faced with a physical stressor and you cannot turn on the right stress response, you are in big trouble. There are two categories of critical hormones secreted during stress. In one disorder, Addison's disease, you cannot secrete glucocorticoids. In another condition called Shy-Drager syndrome, you have difficulty secreting epinephrine and norepinephrine (also called adrenaline and noradrenaline). However, this book is not about this type of stress response.
- If you repeatedly face stressors both physical and psychological, and your stress responses work very well, good for you. The trouble starts when, even after the stressful situation is over, you cannot turn off the stress response. A large percentage of what we think about as stress-related diseases are disorders of excessive stress response.

You need to identify the triggers to stress before you can formulate the solutions or the specific actions you can take to reduce them. This may not happen overnight but you can certainly find solutions over time.

You get 'Neural Dissonance' when you cannot be fully present as a result of unmanaged stress. You can't be fully present at work, and you can't be fully present with your family. The tragedy with Neural Dissonance is that even though you mean to do WELL in both areas, you end up doing POORLY in both . . . because your focus isn't 'clean'. You're robbing both; you're at about 50 percent of the efficiency that you could be.

So, where are YOU living when you experience Neural Dissonance? In other words, are you mixing your life up, trying to do a bunch of things all at once? Where do you feel like you're not putting one hundred percent of your attention into one thing? Where are those times and areas of your life?

First, make a list of all the things you do when you're experiencing Neural Dissonance. This should take about five-ten minutes. Next, get some awareness about what IS important in your life. What are the things you're trying to do when you get Neural Dissonance?

What are the things you want to start putting all your attention into, in focused chunks of time? Go back over your list of being Neural Dissonance areas, and put a star next to the things you need to pull out and focus large chunks of uninterrupted time on. Pick at least one emotional, one mental, and one physical component. Combinations are fine.

Your Three Tanks

An easy metaphor I tell my clients is to imagine that they have to keep different types of fuel ingredients in three tanks. Only when all three tanks are about 60 percent or 80 percent full can you produce a consistent-quality fuel drawn from a mix of all three tanks. The three tanks are outlined below.

Emotional: Family, bonding, intimacy

Mental: Willpower, mental models, beliefs

Physical: Nutrition, diet, sleep, sex

The fuel that runs your life requires input from all three tanks. When any of the tanks runs low:

1) **Your system compensates by using more ingredients from other tanks. The resultant fuel quality is suboptimal. The quality of your output suffers. Creativity is the first thing to go.**
2) **Mental and emotional blinkers come on. Your range of choices becomes reduced.**
3) **Neural Dissonance begins. Amygdala hijacks occur more often.**
4) **Your physiological compensation mechanisms break down. This is the beginning of more acute symptoms or illness.**

Rule of thumb: Have a deliberate routine that keeps your tanks at 60 percent over every four-day busy (working) cycle. For example, your deliberate routine when busy would ensure that you have thirty hours of sleep, twelve meals, eight snacks and eight liters of water over a four-day period. At times of rest keep your tanks 80 percent full. Have routines for everything so you use your five minutes of willpower for emergencies. Also note that after age thirty-five you have a maximum of five minutes of willpower a day.

Wherever you fail to plan, you plan to fail. When you plan you must have a fifteen-minute sequence you can execute otherwise it is wishful thinking. If you cannot break it down to a fifteen-minute sequence that you can practise to perfect your muscle memory, you cannot replicate it.

Nearly 25 percent of people abandon their New Year's resolutions after one week. 60 percent do so within six months. And the average person, get this, makes the same New Year's resolution ten separate times. And 70 percent of organizational change initiatives ultimately fail (if you're a leader, you'll probably feel the sting on this one).

Why does this happen? The reality is most of us are in the dark — not only about setting effective goals but also about staying on track and achieving them. Some people think all you need to do is write down your resolutions around New Year's Day and everything will fall into place. Well, you and I know that is not enough.

> **The key to success is having a powerful process to identify the right priorities and a proven plan to accomplish them, to truly design your life so you are always focused on the things that matter most.**

What does your ideal life look like? Imagine sitting on the same chair you are in right now, but it's now twelve months in the future. Imagine achieving during the last year a level of physical strength and health you have never known before. Wouldn't it feel great to hear others compliment you because they can see the payoffs of such a commitment?

Now imagine your most important relationships. They can be with your spouse, your kids, or your dearest friends. What if those relationships are now deeper and more connected than ever before? Wouldn't it be amazing to overhear the people in these relationships talking about how great you make them feel, about the joy they feel when you are around?

Imagine reviewing your personal and business finances and realizing that you've achieved a level of abundance and security that only a year ago seemed impossible. One year from today, imagine closing your laptop as you get ready to leave your office and exhaling with deep satisfaction and gratitude, knowing you are doing exactly what you are put on this earth to do. Imagine you are making the greatest contribution of your life, and it's acknowledged and celebrated by those around you.

All these things can be real for you. True meaning, freedom, and clarity in every area of your life. Bottom line: the practice of designing your life is not just helpful, it's a prerequisite for happiness.

Psychologists tell us that people who make consistent progress towards meaningful goals live happier and more satisfied lives than those who don't. Regardless of whether you join us for this course or not, if you don't have written goals, let me just encourage you to at least make an appointment on your calendar and identify and list your goals for the coming year. It doesn't take a lot of time.

I'm excited to share with you my goal-achievement process. It took me years to develop, but you can start reaping the same benefits in just a few hours. If you like this book, you will love the online program. It is called "Freedom Formula: Mastering Time, Money, and Leverage in 9 Steps".

All it takes is a few minutes a day for the next eight weeks to make the next year the best you've ever had. We could go faster and blitz the entire course in just a few hours, or we can complete it as scheduled. Either way, this program is designed to guide you through my proven process of creating a plan to ensure that you get clear, get motivated, and most importantly get started on the things that are most important to you right now.

This process has been fine-tuned with over 15,000 of my clients. They've experienced transformation, new-found change, and new-found clarity in their lives. The process works. And this year I made it even better with updated content based on the latest research about goals, motivation, and meaning.

The moment you have exceeded the five minutes of will power you have daily, you will perform at your lowest common denominator. You will go on your DM (default modes/ habits).

The other piece to be aware of is your chunk size. Your chunk size of information is also a DM. Everyone can process 7±2 bits of information per unit of time. The size of each bit will vary. Each bit is a chunk size. In practice, this is how it works:

- Reading speed: Your chunk size can vary from 200 wpm to 50,000 wpm.
- Wardrobe: One person has only one shoe while another has seven shoes. One person has one evening gown while another ten.
- Relationships: One individual has one person in each of seven categories while another has a thousand.

Obviously, each of these individuals will have very different strategies to deal with the level they are operating at and different DMs.

I used to wonder why some of the people who did my personal development programs set goals — and magic happened in their lives. Others did these same programs, also got great clarity and precision — but nothing much changed.

The answer, I realized, was DMs and chunk sizes. So, for example, if I am an accomplished artist or musician and already have a tribe (à all the DMs and chunk sizes are right), all I need to do to become an overnight celebrity is to communicate my value to my tribe.

In contrast, if I am an accomplished artist but I don't have a tribe or following, I have to:

1) **Build a system to collect a tribe**
2) **Have a system to keep in touch**
3) **Develop a marketing and sales system**
4) **Have a front end and back end**
5) **Automate everything**
6) **Be at peace with what I am doing**

Imagine the number of DMs that have to be established. This is a marathon, not a sprint.

Imagine the chunk sizes that will have to change. All this requires effort, energy, resources.

The latter artist will need multiple inputs to do this:

- A manager and publicist
- A personal coach to help her manage her energy, her emotional well-being
- A business strategist.

This is why diets, new year resolutions, etc., fail.

Managing Your Work Environment

Regardless of where you work, you probably deal daily with distractions which are costly. A 2007 study by Basex estimated that distractions cost U.S. businesses $588 billion yearly. This is likely repeated in organizations around the world. After you have been distracted its takes quite a while to get back to work. If you get distracted ten times a day, and you multiply this by ten minutes to return to work, you wonder how you get anything done. You have to learn to cut down distractions if you want to get more done and experience less stress. Without distractions, you can produce more high-quality work, and achieve much more.

Presenteeism

Presenteeism is described as being present at work but not being productive because of mental or physical health reasons. Presenteeism tends to be linked to physical and mental wellness or the lack of it. People miss work for many reasons, legitimate or otherwise. Presenteeism afflicts all business sectors, but some more than others. Much of it revolves around psychological rather than physical ill health. The cost due to presenteeism is likely to be higher than absenteeism! Is this affecting you, your colleagues, or your staff at work?

U.S. companies lose between $200-$300 billion a year due to absenteeism, tardiness, burnout, decreased productivity, worker's compensation claims, increased employee turnover, and medical insurance costs resulting from employee work-related stress.

National Safety Council, Priority Magazine, 1-2/2007

Exercise: Find Your Peak Times

Each one of us has a different 'peak time' or highest-energy time of the day. Some of us are morning people, others have more energy around mid-afternoon, while some people feel their best at night. Most people know instinctively when they are having their 'up' and 'down' times. And you probably don't get just one of these: some people feel up in the morning, down in the afternoon, and up again in the early evening.

What do you need to eliminate to have the following habits/ routines/DMs in place?

- **Identifying the Core Priority**
- **Waking up**
- **Getting ready to work**
- **Winding down before sleep**
- **Dealing with relationships (Work and Personal)**
- **Dealing with Challenges**
- **Problem Solving**
- **Renewal (physical, emotional and mental)**

Compulsive Life	Designed Life
Stress never affects me	I have a routine to minimize negative effects of stress
I never experience dissonance	I have a routine to stay "Present"

To have more impact in your life, join Dr Sundardas for a deep dive Master Class called **"How To Earn Six Figures in Six Months"**, our gift to you. Visit **http://mylife-bydesign.com/masterclass**

https://youtu.be/BKkuGj4YN7Q

9

WHAT ARE YOUR NATURAL ENERGY CYCLES?

The key is in not spending time, but in investing it.

Stephen R. Covey

This is an approach to managing your time and focus to maximize your results. We talked before about special states we get into from time to time where we feel really good and where we're really productive and perform at our 'peak'.

Star athletes call this state *The Zone*. But you can achieve this optimum zone state at work as well as physically, emotionally, and mentally. Getting in the zone is key to maximizing your productivity and fulfillment at work. My 60-60-30 solution is designed to get you into this state so that at the end of every day you look back and feel great about all the results you achieved.

Rising stress levels can cause seriously inappropriate behavior. 13 percent of surveyed workers claimed to have personally committed, or have observed co-workers commit, an act that would be described as "desk rage" — angry or destructive outbursts during work time because of the high levels of stress.
Caravan Opinion Research, 2000

Rhythms In The Body

Our body has many different rhythms or cycles. Many of us are familiar with *Circadian Rhythms*. These are twenty-four-hour cycles of wakefulness and sleep.

Another important cycle is called the *Ultradian Rhythm*, a recurrent period or cycle repeated throughout a twenty-four-hour circadian day. Within the one-day (twenty-four-hour) circadian rhythm, researchers have found shorter, ultradian rhythms. We experience an Ultradian Rhythm every 90 to 120 minutes. You have probably experienced this many times: you were working hard, feeling energized and productive, then you started to tire a bit and lose your focus after a while. This normally occurs after about an hour and a half to two hours. It is a bit different for each person. The Ultradian cycle is the most important cycle for high performance.

Insomnia costs $2,280 per worker in lost productivity, totaling $63.2 million nationally.
Sleep, 2011

Polyphasic Sleep Cycles

Polyphasic sleep means sleeping in cycles of 1.5 hours, and breaking your sleep into multiple, short (1.5-hour) sleep periods throughout the day. It is more efficient than *monophasic* sleep (getting all your sleep in one long chunk). This because with polyphasic sleep only two to five hours of sleep is needed each day.

Keep track of your sleeping and wake-up times. You will need these notes to stay disciplined as you begin to change your sleeping patterns.

The Everyman Cycle consists of one period of core sleep which lasts about three hours and three naps of twenty minutes each spaced evenly throughout the day. When we honor this natural cycle of expending energy and then recovering it, we can get much more done and feel better doing it, over both the short term and longer term.

50 million Americans suffer from sleep problems, many stemming from long work hours, that affect their work, health, relationships, and safety. It also affects their mood and attitude at work. Because of being sleep deprivation:

-- 40 percent said they have become impatient with others at least a few times a month.
-- 27 percent said they frequently found it difficult to concentrate at work.
-- 20 percent felt that their production was below what they had expected.

National Sleep Foundation, March 2008, "Sleep in America"

60-60-30

The idea with 60-60-30 is for us to use sixty-minute chunks of time to focus on a single thing. We put two of these chunks together then we spend thirty minutes completely relaxing and eating a small healthy meal.

One reason this can be so powerful is because if you don't take these breaks, you'll burn your energy reserves and your will-power, and damage the system that allows you to renew. By taking these breaks, you help your renewal system to heal and become more effective.

The 60-minute chunks are actually three cycles of fifteen minutes focused on the task, then a short fifteen-minute break followed by a second round of four cycles of fifteen minutes. I use little timer, set it to forty-five minutes, then put it to the side of my desk. What's great about this is it frees me to completely focus for the next forty-five minutes. I know that I don't need to check emails or voicemails for that forty-five minutes. When it beeps, I set it for fifteen minutes then I go stretch, move around, and in general do something different.

Forcing ourselves to work through with sheer determination as our energy wanes is counterproductive. This is like reading a book when we are tired; we ending up reading the same paragraph over and over again, until we either fall asleep with book (or Nook or Kindle or iPad) in hand, or realize that we must stop. Only then can we regain our focus and comprehension.

Another common strategy when we find ourselves nearing the end of one of our Ultradian Rhythms is to pump ourselves up with caffeine and/or sugar or to 'power through' the energy drop. Or grabbing one of those energy drinks to keep going even when we want to crash.

To sustain peak performance, we need to manage our energy throughout the day. We allow our body and mind to renew by taking periodic breaks every ninety minutes. By working with our natural (down) cycles, we can become many times more effective and productive throughout the day.

Many of us must have heard about the sad demise in 2010 of Ranjan Das, from Mumbai, India, who at forty-two years old was the youngest CEO of an MNC (SAP-Indian Subcontinent) in India. He was very active in sports, a fitness freak, and a marathon runner. It was common to see him run on Bandra's Carter Road. Just after Diwali, on 21st Oct 2010, he returned home from his gym after a workout, collapsed with a massive heart attack, and died. He is survived by his wife and two very young kids.

It was certainly a wake-up call for corporate India, let alone corporate Asia. However, it was even more disastrous for the runners amongst us. Since Ranjan was an avid marathoner (he ran the Chennai Marathon in Feb 2009), the question arises as to why an exceptionally active, athletic person succumbed to a heart attack at forty-two years of age.

Sleep deprivation is now costing U.S. companies $63.2 billion a year in lost productivity. Exhaustion makes employees less-efficient, even in the time it takes to read email. They are also more irritable and more likely to explode.
Harvard Medical School, 2013

Was It The Stress?

Das himself had mentioned that he faced a lot of stress, but that is a common element in most of our lives. It is commonly accepted that being fit allows you to conquer the bad effects of stress, so I doubt if stress was the cause of his untimely death.

However, there was one line in the reports that everyone missed: Ranjan used to make do with four-five hours of sleep daily. Das himself had admitted that he would have loved to get more sleep (and that he was not proud of his ability to manage without sleep, contrary to what others extolled).

I have outlined some key points below in the hope it will save lives.

- Short sleep durations (<five or five-six hours) increase risk for high blood pressure (BP) by 350 percent to 500 percent compared to those who slept longer than six hours per night. As you know, high BP kills. Paper published in 2009.
- Young people (25-49 years of age) are twice as likely to get high BP if they sleep less. Paper published in 2006.
- Individuals who slept less than five hours a night had a three-fold increased risk of heart attacks. Paper published in 1999.
- Complete and partial lack of sleep increased the blood concentrations of High-Sensitivity C-Reactive Protein (hs-cRP), the strongest predictor of heart attacks. Even after getting adequate sleep later, the levels stayed high!!
- Just one night of sleep loss increases very toxic substances in body such as Interleukin-6 (IL-6), Tumor Necrosis Factor-Alpha (TNF-alpha), and cRP. They increase risks of many medical conditions, including cancer, arthritis, and heart disease. Paper published in 2004.
- Sleeping for <=five hours per night leads to a 39 percent increase in heart disease. Sleeping for <=six hours per night leads to an 18 percent increase in heart disease. Paper published in 2006.

Lack of space here does not allow me to detail the ideal sleep architecture, but here's an outline. Sleep consists of two stages: REM (Rapid Eye Movement) and non-REM. The former helps in mental consolidation while the latter helps in physical repair and rebuilding. During the night, you alternate between REM and non-REM stages four-five times.

The earlier part of sleep is mostly non-REM. During that period, your pituitary gland releases growth hormones that repair your body. This part of sleep is when Human Growth Hormone (HGH) is naturally generated. It normally occurs between ten pm to twelve midnight. If you are not asleep by this point, what happens is that you generate *cortisol*, a stress hormone that has the long-term effects of accelerating ageing and leading to the production of toxic substances like IL-6, TNF-alpha, and cRP.

Traditional Chinese Medicine (TCM) has the concept of *chi* (life force) and its movement in different *meridians* (channels) at different times. The Liver Meridian is particularly active from 1 am to 3 am. If you are asleep during this period, your Liver Meridian can properly detoxify your liver as well as your *mesenchymal matrix* (deep cellular nutrient and detoxification system). If you are not asleep, this function is thwarted and your natural cellular detoxification mechanisms start shutting down. This prepares your body for the development of severe and chronic diseases.

The latter part of sleep is more and more REM type. The latter part of sleep is more important to ensure you are mentally alert during the day. No wonder then that when an alarm 'forces' you to wake up after only five-six hours of sleep (lack of REM sleep), you are mentally irritable throughout the day. And if you have slept for less than five hours (lack of non-REM sleep), your body is in a complete physical mess. You are tired throughout the day; you move like a zombie, and your immunity is way down. (I've been there, done that.)

Unfortunately, Ranjan Das was not alone when it comes to not getting enough sleep. Many of us are doing exactly the same, perhaps out of ignorance.

In 2007, I developed a devastating infection called rheumatic fever and experienced heart failure (my heart function dropped to thirty percent). This was at a period in my life when I was eating well, exercising well (perhaps too well: I was averaging almost twelve hours weekly in aerobics, weights, and martial arts) — but sleeping only five hours a day and working at least fifty hours a week. There was a month I worked right through, non-stop; that was when the infection struck.

My blood profile was perfect except for elevated CRP, Creatinine Kinase, and the infection marker. All the other markers of heart disease such as cholesterol, triglycerides, glucose, sodium, and potassium were perfect.

It took me almost two years to get back to normal. After almost forty years of being sleep deprived, I learnt how to sleep well and deeply.

What To Do Next?

Identify your core life habits. How many of them are robust and help you stay well? How many of them are toxic and contribute to disease and reduced function?

Identify what you need to eliminate or change:

Mood swings
Cannot say "No"
Chronic overwork
Confused priorities
Frequent mood swings
Infrequent or no exercise
Consistently overcommitted
Eating irregularly and poorly
Frequent feelings of being overwhelmed
Sleeping less than seven hours a day
Unable to stay on track with goals
Inability to follow through with commitments
Consistently troubleshooting at work and at home
Insufficient or no time spent with life partner or family

Compulsive Life	Designed Life
I can get by with little sleep	I am clear that my brain works best with optimal sleep
I thrive on the thrill of excitement	I thrive on positive habits

To have more impact in your life, join Dr Sundardas for a deep dive Master Class called **"How To Earn Six Figures in Six Months"**, our gift to you.
Visit **http://mylife-bydesign.com/masterclass**

B) DISCARD

6) Create Firewalls To Protect Your Boundaries And Learn To Say No To What Doesn't Serve You

https://youtu.be/DMRJ606SXNU

10

CAN YOU DANCE TO CHANGE?

It is the time you have wasted for your rose
that makes your rose so important.

Antoine de Saint-Exupéry, **The Little Prince**

Pioneering family-therapy expert Virginia Satir developed a model of how individuals experience change.

According to her model, during the process of change we predictably move through the following stages: Old Status Quo, Chaos, Integration, and New Status Quo.

The Satir Change Model describes what happens at each stage in terms of feelings, thinking, performance, and physiology. When you're aware of this framework you can improve how you process change and help others process change as well.

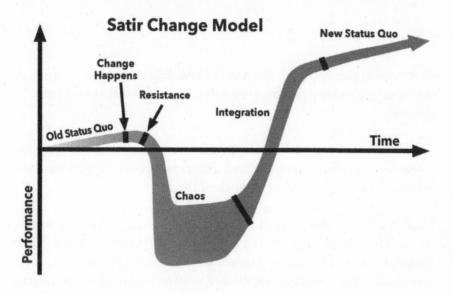

The Five Stages Of The Satir Change Model

The Old Status Quo

You are in a familiar place. Your performance pattern is consistent. You pretty much know what to do and how to react. Implicit and explicit rules underlie behavior. It's the 'same old world' you live in.

The Foreign Element

A Foreign Element threatens the stability of the familiar. Initially you may deal with the impending change element by denying its validity, avoiding the issue, or blaming someone for causing the problem. These resistance-to-change tactics are accompanied by unconscious physical and emotional responses that can have adverse effects. Resistance clogs awareness and conceals the issues highlighted by the Foreign Element.

Chaos

At this point you enter the unknown. Prevailing norms are challenged, old expectations may no longer be valid, and old behaviors may not be possible.

The loss of belonging and identity triggers anxiousness and vulnerability. These may give rise to stress-related disorders. You may experience lack of concentration and focus for much of the day.

Until you accept the Foreign Element, your life seems to turn upside down. The Chaos stage is vital to the transformation process. Some things that you try work and others do not. Although chaos can be a very creative time, you may experience its stress and urgency more than the thrill of creativity.

The Transforming Idea

Eventually you may discover a Transforming Idea that shows how the Foreign Element can benefit you. You become excited and inspired. A new identity may emerge with a very different framework of operations. The transforming idea gives you a new perspective of what is going on. You begin to see a way out of the chaos.

Integration

This is when things start to come together for you. You check out new ways of behaving and thinking. You learn rapidly and make progress. New learning is always punctuated with lots of mistakes; progress occurs in fits and starts. Soon you learn what works and what does not. Your skill level rises and you become more optimistic about the outcomes. You sense that you are moving toward something new. Your performance exceeds the levels you were at before the introduction of the foreign element.

The New Status Quo

Well-conceived and well-assimilated change will result in a higher level of homeostasis and improved performance than in the old status quo.

A healthy change leaves you calm and alert. You are more centered with more erect posture and deeper breathing. You feel free to observe and communicate what is really happening. A sense of accomplishment and possibility permeates the atmosphere.

At this stage, as you master your new skills, your performance begins to level off. You continue to get excellent results with less concentration and attention. You feel good about how rapidly you are learning. Armed with new skills, knowledge, and confidence, you turn your attention toward other important areas of your life.

Eventually, your new skills become automated default modes and reflexive. Your learning becomes assumptions and expectations. The new status quo becomes the old status quo with the passage of time.

And the change cycle begins again.

With respect to different changes you may be in different stages. You may be in a late-status-quo stage in one area of your life, and in chaos in another area because of unexpected changes.

Of course, things can happen before you are ready for change. Something unexpected can happen while you are still practicing the transforming idea from an earlier change. It may arrive when you are in the middle of chaos.

Each stage of the Satir Change Model has a purpose. Even though our responses seem painful and confusing, there are sound reasons for each stage.

Change Levels

There are different levels of change. The more the required levels of change the harder the transition. In a conceptual framework from Neuro-Linguistic Programming popularized by Robert Dilts, we have the idea of Neurological Change Sequence.

Fig: Neurological Levels of Change

In a program called "Success Permissions" that I teach, we do a 'phobia cure'. People who have had a phobia all their lives find they no longer have a phobia after that ten-minute process. Phobia cures can take classic psychology a few months to a few years — and that is only for one specific habit change.

Then in another part of that program, we help individuals overcome *deep-imprint traumas,* i.e. those that occurred during ages zero-seven. Classic psychological work can take five to ten years to do this type of change work.

These changes happen at the levels of Values/Beliefs and Identity. Change can occur at a few levels. For example, you are a smoker and you have decided to quit. By the time you do this you have gone through a few stages:

- From unconscious incompetence to conscious incompetence that you don't know how to stop smoking (Stairway of Learning)
- From Pre-contemplation to Contemplation to Ready to Change (The Stages of Change)

Then you start getting ready to learn about how to quit smoking. If your smoking falls at the level of Environment, you change the people you hang out with to stop smoking.

If you are smoking at the level of Behavior, you learn a new habit and in twenty-one days you are done.

If you are smoking because you identify yourself as a smoker, you need a new identity before you will change. This will be more challenging to change. Very often people join a new religion or a special club that gives them this new identity.

The classic example of this is in the Bible with Saul, who used to persecute Christians. On the road to Damascus, he develops hysterical blindness and hears a voice saying, "Saul why do you persecute me?" He has a conversion experience, becomes a Christian, and now calls himself Paul. He can see again.

So the Satir Change Model incorporates all of the above. The change sequence is broken up into stages. However, each stage except for The Old Status Quo incorporates multiple change points.

For instance, this book *Life by Design* was written very differently from my other books. I spent twenty years (ages 25-45) thinking about writing this book. (Fortunately, I had my early notes.)

I developed an online program that took approximately three months to develop. It took me 1.5 years of learning how to create online programs before I could do this. It took another three years to learn how to promote programs online. All these are diverse skill sets. I had to contemplate going online from ages thirty-five to forty-four before I was ready to do something at age forty-four.

So if we look at the book and the online program in the context of the Satir Change Model, it took me twenty years of change, learning, and growth before I got ready to write the book, and create an online program and launch it.

Challenges in Change

I was contemplating the challenges I would experience when I was learning or doing things I had never done before. I used to get angry and frustrated before. I would ask myself, "Why is it so hard? Others don't seem to have such challenges."

Then it struck me. Most people don't make any changes in their lives. They do the same thing, day in, day out. Their lives run out while they are still contemplating the possibility they might change.

So I worked out a rough equation. Let's assume you make a major change. It takes one year. Every major change that takes about a year will have five major blocks or challenges. Minor changes will take four months and involve maybe two challenges.

This morning, I got a message from a team leader I was working with on a major project that he was leaving the company and team. We had been working on this for almost 1.5 years. I was really cool about the matter. Why you may ask?

I am currently working on six projects. Three are major, three are smaller. So I can expect twenty-one blocks or challenges, approximately two challenges per month in the course of a year. This knowledge totally changed my perspective.

If you do nothing different, your pathway is smooth. You are not walking your true path. So challenges are a measure of how you are learning and growing. The latest brain research has shown that doing this keeps your brain young if you keep doing it up to your fifties. Note that this is not fire-fighting but genuinely learning new things.

Managing the Change Process

Take care of yourself and stay healthy. Remember: This will not last. You will eventually have a Transforming Idea.

You may want to avoid Chaos at all costs. Naturally you may want things to remain unchanged.

View the Foreign Element as an harbinger (early warning) of Change. Ask yourself what it means? Look for at least three different ways of explaining the new inputs and verify them experimentally.

Give yourself credit for recognizing and accepting agent. This is more useful than living in denial. Acknowledge that you are in Chaos. Spend some time observing and learning from your internal reactions.

Remember that Chaos is a natural part of the change process. When you are in Chaos it's okay to feel out of control. Also remember that Chaos is necessary. New ideas of often emerge from Chaos-induced urgency. These new perspectives help you make sense of the Foreign Element.

Identify the frameworks challenged by the Foreign Element. Clearly stating this framework may help to move on to the next stage which is identifying the Transforming Idea.

Consider adjusting how you measure your performance. Give yourself time to adjust when you are coping with change in Chaos. Try not to make irreversible long-term decisions. Your judgment may not be at its best right now. Get support from other people. Talk to others about what is going on with you. Be aware of what is going on for others undergoing the change process. Mentor each other. Share ideas and experiences. Stay grounded in the present.

Reduce/Eliminate Interruptions

Consider the many interruptions that occurred in your last workday. There may have been interruptions in the office that unexpectedly demanded your attention. Everyday interruptions at work can be a key barrier to managing your time effectively and can be an obstacle to your success.

Just a handful of small interruptions can rob you of success in your work and life. Continually re-engaging to successfully complete complex work after interruptions can be challenging.

You can control interruptions by planning for them both in terms of factoring time for essential interruptions and non-essential interruptions in your daily schedule. Listed below are ideas on how to prevent and reduce interruptions.

1. Log Records

Keep track in a log of interruptions you experience in a day. This becomes essential if you are constantly interrupted or pushed off schedule by interruptions. Record every interruption you experience, and note the person interrupting you; the date and time it occurs; what the interruption is; and whether it was valid or urgent. Once you have recorded the interruptions for a week, sit down with your log and analyze the information. Which interruptions were valid and which were not?

The Interrupters Log

Person	Date/Time	Description of Interruption	Valid	Urgent

2. Figure Out What Matters

Were all the interruptions necessary? Could any have been deferred to a routine meeting? If so, deal with them politely but assertively. To analyze and conquer the interruptions you find in your log firstly look at whether an interruption was valid or not.

3. Use Your Phone Well

If you cannot be interrupted have an assistant deal with messages for you or use voice mail to screen calls.

4. Do Breath Control

When interrupted, it's easy to get caught up in the agenda of the person who is interrupting; he will undoubtedly feel his request is urgent. Generally, most interruptions are not really crisis-driven. Pause, re-assess the situation accurately, and react suitably.

5. Say "No"

It's usually acceptable to say "No" to requests or tasks if you are busy, when someone else can handle it, if it is not an important task, or if it can be done later. When this is the case, saying "No" in a courteous and sincere way, followed by a short explanation, is the best course of action to take.

6. Announce Your Timing

Let people know in advance of your availability. Make sure that people know that during your 'Unavailable Time' they should interrupt you only if they have to.

7. "Invites Only"

Schedule regular check-in times for individuals you talk to most often. You can cover everything at one time if you ask them to keep a prioritized list of what they need to discuss. Force yourself to do the same.

8. Out-of-Control Interruptions

There are interruptions you simply cannot control. Most people are happy to schedule a more convenient time, but when this does not work, quickly set the parameters by saying something like, "I have only five minutes to talk about this right now", and stick to it.

9. Control Internet Use

Browsing the Web can suck up enormous amounts of time and it's easy to get lost for twenty minutes or more when we start looking on the Internet for one thing.

- **Read The News** - In order to avoid being distracted during the day, visit news sites or read newspapers before work, so that you know the news.
- **Shut Your Internet Browser** – When not using it keep you Internet browser closed so you are not distracted.
- **Use Tailored Software** – You can specify which websites you want to block using software application like **Freedom** and **Anti-Social**, and set a timer for how long you want the block to remain active.

- **Take Internet Breaks** – Taking little breaks, especially after working for an hour or more in deep concentration, allows you to re-focus on work with renewed energy
- **Other People** – Close your door to keep people from casually stopping by. Talk to the noisy colleague who may not be aware he/she is distracting you.

10. Take Care of Yourself

Get enough sleep, watch your diet (avoid heavy lunches), and stay hydrated. When you are tired, go for a walk, get some fresh air, and move your body. You can have a productive day only when you are well rested. You can choose to assess how well you are meeting your goals and targets by developing your own monitoring system for your exercise, nutrition, rest, and work schedules.

Compulsive Life	Designed Life
I am excited by change	I make sure that I have routines to negotiate change
I change in reaction to circumstances	I change to meet my core priority
I always plan to finish on time	I always build in buffer time in my planning

---

The Websites below provide more information on making positive changes in your health status:

www.sundardasnaturopathy.com

www.blog.drsundardas.com

C) IMPLEMENT

Effortless Implementation

Whether our goal is to plan a birthday party for our child, climb up the ladder at work, or complete a project at work, we tend to think of implementation as hard work, something we need to force and make happen.

However, the Life Design model is very different. We don't need to force implementation; because of the prior stages of Evaluate and Discard, a system has been created for removing obstacles and making implementation effortless.

These three elements — Evaluate, Discard, Implement — are parts of an iterative, cyclical process that moves you towards higher levels of performance and personal satisfaction.

In Chapter 1, we spoke about how to keep your shoe rack in order. Do this in an organized fashion and it feels effortless; do this in a haphazard, fitful fashion, however, and it morphs into a nightmare scenario.

To achieve this effortless state, all the elements required of the previous two stages have been well explored and the necessary steps clearly delineated. Appropriate resources have been acquired; timelines have taken into consideration the flow of energy and resources, and how people operate.

While compulsive types force execution of plans, those who understand the Designed Life implement effortlessly. When all unnecessary details have been eliminated, habits automated, and sequences streamlined, implementation becomes a seamless piece of the whole. We naturally want to do things the easy way.

In the next section, we look at the elements and the sequence required to make things effortless when implementing. This is the basis for the well-designed life.

C) IMPLEMENT

7) Schedule The Goals And Targets You Need To Achieve (Develop your Prioritized To-Do List)

https://youtu.be/-6bCyiKVLdo

11

WHAT IS THE STEP-BY-STEP APPROACH TO LIFE DESIGN?

Unfortunately, the clock is ticking, the hours are going by. The past increases, the future recedes. Possibilities decreasing, regrets mounting.

Haruki Murakami, **Dance Dance Dance**

Now let us discuss the detailed steps to implement a well-designed life.

A person who works with a "messy" or cluttered desk spends, on average, 1.5 hours per work-day, 7.5 hours per work-week, looking for things or being distracted by things. "Out of sight, out of mind." When it's in sight, it's in mind.

The *Productivity Ladder* is a powerful tool to help you prioritize your highest-leverage activities:

- High lifetime value
- High dollar per hour
- Low dollar per hour
- Zero or negative value.

High lifetime value includes building relationships with people we want to do business with in the future. Make a list of the things you do daily that fall into these four zones.

Next, draw three overlapping circles (see the image on right):

1. Represents your strengths
2. Represents high lifetime value
3. Represents high dollar value

Where all these circles overlap (X) is where you want to spend as much of your time as possible. When you do, you'll maximize your results, and maximize your fulfilment.

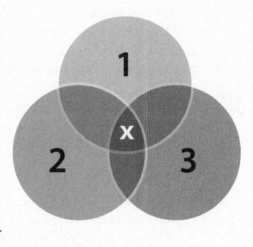

Go ahead and write down two-three activities that fall in that overlapping space. Next, if you want to set yourself up for success, it's important that you 'clean the grill', just like a restaurant does at the end of the day.

If you don't clean the grill of a restaurant at the end of the day, the grill gets all mucked up, and when you come in in the morning you're not really ready to start cooking. Cleaning the grill in business means you close any 'loose loops' at the end of the day, so the next morning you can start with a clear head and clean focus. One simple way to clean the grill is to get enough sleep at night. This is a way to clean up your 'physical grill'.

So when you're ready to wrap up work you've done in some area, set it up so the next time you want to work on it, you're ready to go.

The Four Quadrants of Time Management

In Steven Covey's bestselling book, *The 7 Habits of Highly Effective People*, he explains how every activity we do during the day can be put into one of four quadrants:

1. Urgent and Important
2. Not Urgent and Important
3. Urgent and Not Important
4. Not Urgent and Not Important

The characteristics associated with these four quadrants are:

1. URGENT & IMPORTANT

   - Stress
   - Burn-out
   - Crisis management
   - Always putting out fires

2. NOT URGENT & IMPORTANT

   - Vision, perspective
   - Balance
   - Discipline
   - Control
   - Few crises

3. URGENT & NOT IMPORTANT

   - Short-term focus
   - Crisis management
   - Reputation as a chameleon character
   - See goals and plans as worthless
   - Feel victimized, out of control
   - Shallow or broken relationships

4. NOT URGENT & NOT IMPORTANT

- Total irresponsibility
- Fired from jobs
- Dependent on others or institutions for basics

Prioritization Exercise (Developing Your Prioritized To-Do List):

Write down what want to achieve in your life over the next ten years. (Most people aren't used to thinking in such large time frames.) Where would you like to be ten years from now personally and professionally? What activities could you do right now to reach your goals? Where do your strengths and enjoyment overlap with high-lifetime-value and high-dollar-per-hour activities?

The Two Ingredients of Success

There are really only two ingredients of success. If you are missing an ingredient, or you don't have enough of one, you are bound to fail. On the other hand, if you have both ingredients in abundance, success is practically guaranteed. These two ingredients are:

1. Knowing the right things to do
2. Prioritizing those actions and doing them

Sometimes you know the right things to do and you may be prioritizing them, but obstacles keep getting in the way of achieving results. In this case, you need to know what to do in order to overcome the obstacles, and again this boils down to knowing the right things to do.

If you're not successful, then either you don't know what things to do or you're not prioritizing them. People tend to not be very good at prioritizing (e.g. they want to grow their business, but they spend all their time managing day-to-day operations and spend no time on growth).

The 80/20 Rule

We covered the 80/20 Rule or Pareto Principle earlier (page 65). It says that 80 percent of the results come from 20 percent of the actions you take, while 20 percent of results are produced by 80 percent of the actions you take. Most times you will find it to be true.

Most people get only 20 percent of the results because they spend time doing the 80 percent that is not important. They never get around to doing the most important actions. If you focus on what matters most first, you will easily get results faster.

Let's call these important actions (20 percent) your 'High-Priority Actions' and the rest of the actions (80 percent) your 'Low-Priority Actions'.

Commit to doing high-priority actions first. Manage obstacles to high-priority actions. Come around to the low-priority actions only after you've completed the high-priority ones.

The exercise below will help you to apply 80/20 Rule. It will save you hours or days of work!

Exercise – Applying the 80/20 Rule

1. **Identify your core priority. Thereafter choose a goal or intention that moves you in that direction. A measurable goal such as "Have 50+ clients by June fifteenth" works best, but you can also do this exercise on an intention, such as "Get more clients". Write down your goal or intention now.**

2. **Brainstorm what it would take to achieve your goals. Remain open to new ideas. Don't censor your ideas. Write down everything you can think of. Make a list now.**

3. **Now ask yourself, "If I took only 20 percent of these actions, which ones would likely produce 80 percent of the results?" Circle each action which fits in the top 20-percent category. If you don't know where to start, experiment.**

Effective Scheduling:
Planning to Make the Best Use of Your Time

It's the end of another busy working day and, even though you came into the office early and left late, you don't feel as if you've accomplished anything significant.

It's all too easy for this to happen. You can easily be busy all day without making any progress on high-priority projects and goals because of all the endless meetings, frequent interruptions, and urgent last-minute tasks that happen.

That's why it's so important to know how to schedule your time properly. In this chapter, we'll look at what you can do to manage your time so that you can do work that matters and still have a life after work.

Scheduling Importance

Scheduling is the art of planning your activities so that you can efficiently achieve what you want in the time available.

Most people don't use time well; in fact, they waste it. Scheduling helps you think about what you want to do. It keeps you on track.

1. Optimize Your Time Management.

Make sure that you schedule regularly, and update your schedule appropriately. You can use appropriate tools either online or offline (like pen and paper) to build your schedule. Always schedule high-priority tasks first.

2. Ensure That You Can Complete Essential Tasks As Intended.

Next, block in the actions you absolutely must take to do a good job or to achieve targets for your business. This will be how you measure your performance. Allow time for crucial interactions with key people in your life, at work or personally.

3. Plan For The Unexpected.

Schedule some extra time to cope with emergencies. The more unpredictable your job, the more you need to plan for the unexpected.

4. Avoid Over-Commitment.

Learn to say no to anything that detracts, distracts or derails you from what matters.

5. Work Steadily Toward Your Personal And Career Goals.

Ensure that your scheduling allows you to move in the intended direction you wish to move as you steadily achieve your goals. At the end of the day, you should be able to hit your personal targets and goals.

6. Ensure You Have Time For Personal And Social Needs.

This will make sure that you can continue to be efficient and you don't burn out. This journey is a marathon and not a one hundred-meter sprint.

7. Schedule Discretionary Time

Use the gap that is not scheduled in your planner as "discretionary time" to do what needs to be done. Create an appropriate schedule based on your prioritized To-Do List.

Step 8: Review Activities

If, you find that you have little or no discretionary time available by the time you reach Step 7 above, you need to review steps two to four. You need to relook at all of the tasks you've listed and see if they are absolutely necessary.

Maximizing the leverage you can achieve by delegating. Delegate, outsource or use technology to automate as much as possible. This will free you up to achieve your goals. Renegotiate if your discretionary time is still limited.

The Easiest Way To Manage Time For Greater Productivity

There are various methods you can use to manage time for greater productivity. By now, you should know that preparation is key to becoming successful. If you are seeking the simplest method to manage time for greater productivity, then be sure to allow yourself enough time to discover it. Once you do, arrange time to design for a fulfilling life. Typically, one hour is a decent duration to achieve this goal.

You're now ready to get into the work at hand. However, first we will cover a few positive practices. This way you are as prepared as possible the moment you begin to manage time for greater productivity.

To prepare to manage time for greater productivity are, you should be: planning in advance; scheduling events in fifteen-minute chunks; and anticipating emergencies or building in buffer time. Together these tips create a dependable core for your legwork.

For the one hour that you put aside to prepare for Life Design for greater productivity, focus on planning in three- or five-year chunks, planning backwards from five years to the present, and planning for tasks to be done in fifteen-minute chunks. The major mistake that people make while looking to manage time for greater productivity is disregarding preparation. Now that you are informed, be sure to designate one hour of preparation prior to planning.

Please make sure you do not skip this section of the procedure. Choose to get ready the painless way so you experience all the following benefits: knowing your sequence of actions, i.e. what to do next; having the time to learn the necessary skills; and being able to plan for the unexpected. You also benefit in additional ways such as having achievable goals, getting peace of mind, and experiencing the thrill of victory.

If you invest in Life Design for a fulfilling life, then you may discover that it's much easier than you would have anticipated. The right preparation prepares you to become completely prepared. This results in planning for the unexpected, experiencing the thrill of victory, and having a clear sense of direction. These benefits lead you to effectively manage time for greater productivity. Having said that, don't feel the urge to rush through the training; all these benefits are equally essential.

When watching people who effectively manage time for greater productivity, it may be easy to believe that they have some magical energy or know some special trick that permits them to become a relentless achiever. However, there's no secret. Life Design for greater productivity merely requires an individual who's focused, relentless, and enlightened. By taking the time to be certain that your efforts are really working, you will be able to manage time for greater productivity at a fast pace.

In closing, the simplest method for Life Design for greater productivity is to perform all the tasks laid out here. Cutting corners is not worth the energy; it should be avoided while planning for a fulfilling life.

Devote your efforts to the first part of the procedure; it makes you more productive. The truth is that the one hour you spend here is a tiny price to pay for an activity with such impact as planning regularly. So, make the commitment, spend the required amount of time, and you can be designing a great life!

How do you go about creating inevitable success? It's one of the most important concepts I've ever discovered. It's the evolution of Goal Setting. It's about creating the conditions so success becomes INEVITABLE, so that success happens automatically.

Here's an example. If you want to start going to the gym every day, one thing you can do is find an accountability partner who shows up every day at your doorstep, expecting you to go. This makes success much likelier than just setting the goal of going to the gym.

How can you set up conditions in your life so that the outcomes you want in your personal and professional life become inevitable?

Let us assess how you manage your time. If you answer this honestly you will find out how efficient you are.

Are you looking at your key results, assessing your major opportunities? Are you aware of where you should be focusing to get the most results from your efforts?

How about whether your physical appearance and presentation is up to scratch? If it is not then you may end up losing time, money, and resources because you are not acting appropriately for the environment.

Make sure to incorporate the appropriate physical, emotional, and mental components required. What would you need to focus on? Who would you need to meet? Remember to include 'on-ramps' and 'off-ramps' (discussed in the following chapter). Every ninety days, review this and tweak as necessary.

Finally, let's talk about setting up your physical environment for maximum creativity and productivity. Some people like to create brand new things, others are creative by taking an existing system to the next level.

There's a lot of factors to your physical environment. Either work standing up, as I do, or get an ergonomic, high-quality chair. Get a nice big monitor. Make sure your keyboard and mouse are in positions that don't create stress in your wrists, arms, etc. Turn off alerts that tell you when you have new email or voicemail.

Make a list of the things you can do to create an environment for optimum creativity and productivity. Are you making maximum use of your in-house and out-sourced resources?

Next, let's look at creating your ideal day. Look at the biggest goals you have for the next three-ten years, and look at what you want to accomplish over the next three-twelve months that support that. Then look at what kind of day would support getting these shorter-term goals met.

> ### Find out how to get more training at
> ### www.thefreedom-formula.com

C) IMPLEMENT

8) Ensure That You Have The Right Habits In Place To Achieve Your Targets

https://youtu.be/nkYxO3F1bI8

12

HOW TO CREATE YOUR PERSONALIZED SUCCESS RITUAL

For every minute spent organizing, an hour is earned.

Benjamin Franklin

The rarest and most valuable form of action is 'Deliberate Repetition'. This technique will help you get the most from the efforts you put into your life. One of the highest-leverage ways to use Deliberate Repetition is with your Personalized Success Ritual.

I recommend doing it first thing in the day. Why? Your morning sets your context for the day; it sets the 'frame' by which you judge everything else that happens during the day. If you set the context in the morning right, you'll have a great day. If you have a great day, it'll set the context up for a great week, month, etc.

Your inner game — how you're feeling about yourself — is the highest leverage in your life. Your morning ritual can really help you get into a great inner-game state.

When planning your ritual, think of what would make you strong physically, emotionally, and mentally. My morning ritual includes drinking water, exercising for twenty minutes, taking a bath, and having a healthy, energizing breakfast.

After I've done my morning ritual, I feel clear, I'm centered, and I'm ready for my day. I'm ready for anything that comes at me. I feel like nothing can really knock me off.

When I don't do my morning ritual, I feel like I'm in reactive mode all day. I still get a lot done, but I'm not nearly as productive, and by the end of the day I can feel pretty worn out.

Find a first meal of the day that really works for you. Consider making it as organic and raw as possible. Include some protein as well.

Write down the conditions that need to be in place for you to focus during the "First two hours of your day", and 'flow-chart' the actual steps in your new ritual. Imagine how it's going to go; see if you forgot any steps. Then go out there and do it. If you're getting stuck on a particular step, fix it or remove it. Improve your ritual a little every week. It'll pay HUGE dividends.

The key to designing the new habit is as follows:

1) **Chunk it down into fifteen-minute bits.**
2) **Make sure every minute in that piece is carefully planned.**
3) **Ensure that your environment is designed so that everything is in place for the new habit to take off.**
4) **Ensure that timing includes preparing to start and winding down.**
5) **Ensure that your brain does not get tired going through each piece.**
6) **Note that every new habit takes twenty-one days to form.**
7) **Rest for twenty-one days before starting a new habit.**
8) **Have a clear and compelling picture of your life with these new habits in place.**

Plan your morning ritual intentionally, step by step. Plan the 'wind-up' to your ritual — that's the ten-fifteen minutes before you start your ritual. Plan the ritual itself, and be super specific. If you're drinking water, how are you going to remind yourself, where are you going to get it, etc. Plan your exercise, your first meal, etc. Finally, plan the 'wind-down' to your ritual: how you'll come back into the stream of the rest of your day. Do your morning ritual every day for the next seven days.

How Does Happiness Relate To Productivity?
-- 31 percent higher productivity
-- 37 percent higher sales
-- Creativity 3 times higher.
Happiness at Work Survey, Nic Marks, nef (new economics foundation, London) 20twelve

If you have a way of monitoring your productivity, use it. Keep track of your productivity before and after the new habit forms. Often, as you notice the continued gains, this provides the motivation to continue making changes. Plan to do your most productive work in the first two hours of your work day. The rest of the day should have rituals focused on all the necessary follow-ups that are part and parcel of any business.

Whether we want to admit it, we are all creatures of habit. 99 percent of the things we'll say, feel, and think today are the same things we said, felt, and thought yesterday.

It's almost impossible to 'remember' to do something different when we need to remember it. The answer is to practice it and make it a routine… so when we need to do it, it's automatic. This way we leverage our nature as creatures of habit, for our benefit.

If something is the most important thing, if it's the thing that gets you the highest results, it makes sense to do it every day and make it a habit.

To create a successful new routine, you need to plan it IN DETAIL. When you plan it out, you'll see it's a series of steps. You'll soon find the most efficient sequence for you.

Change is always uncomfortable. If you understand that, you can make the process of learning a new habit more painless and comfortable. The most important rule for learning a new habit is that you must repeat it for twenty-one days. When you do so, you will initiate a process called *neural canalization*, literally forming new brain pathways.

In addition, when you are learning a new habit, it is important to plan every step down to the last minute and rehearse it. This then provides your brain a template as how to do it. Make sure that you reserve your limited will power to initiate the whole process. (Why is this last important? Remember that after age thirty-five you have only five minutes of will power daily, so use it sparingly, and for the right things such as jump-starting new habits and processes.) Thereafter, the sequence should kick in.

Routines of Olympians

For years before Michael Phelps became the gold medalist at the 2008 Beijing Olympics, he followed the same routine at every race. He arrived two hours early. He warmed up according to a precise pattern that included an eight-hundred-meter mixer, a fifty-meter freestyle, kicking six hundred meters with kickboard, pulling a buoy four hundred meters, and more. Thereafter he would dry off, put in his earphones, and sit (not lie) on the massage table. He would not speak to his coach Bob Bowman until the race was over.

Phelps would put on his race suit at the forty-five-minute mark (i.e., forty-five minutes before the race). At the thirty-minute mark, he would get into the warm-up pool and swim six hundred to eight hundred meters. He would walk to the ready room at the ten-minute mark. He would sit alone with two empty seats next to him, one for his goggles on one side and one for his towel on the other.

When he was called for his race, he would walk to the blocks. There his precise routine was two stretches: first a straight-leg stretch and then a stretch with a bent knee. He would always start with his left leg followed by his right. Then the right ear bud would come out. When his name was called, he would take out the left ear-bud. He would step on the block, always from the left side and dry the block. Then he would stand and move his arms in a precise, unique fashion.

As the same routine is practiced day in, day out, it takes over. Phelps was going through the same winning race over and over again. In other words, he was repeating what he had done numerous times in training and winning. The Olympics was no exception.

Forming Habits That Support Your Success

This model is the most powerful concept I've ever learned when it comes to productivity and getting the most out of yourself. It's called Habit Formation, and it's a synthesis between Zen and Systems Thinking. Weird, I know. The most important and powerful state we can be in is the state called Awareness.

Awareness is when we remember we're alive. We zoom out for a second and see the bigger picture. Imagine you get in a major car accident, and it shocks you so much that you call up all the people you love and tell them you love them. That's Awareness.

The rarest and most precious form of ENERGY we have is Will Power. We get a tiny bit of it each day, and we often waste it on things that aren't that important (like holding back our true emotions).

Now, it takes about twenty-one days to form a new habit. If you do something every day, it'll take on a life of its own after twenty-one days.

Days 1-7 is the first phase. I call it Defying Inertia. Inertia is the innate resistance to change. Everything inside you will tell you, "No, I don't want to do that!"

Days 8-14 is the second phase. I call it Resistance. You're no longer defiant, but you still have to push through. You don't naturally feel like doing it yet.

Days fifteen-twenty-one is the third phase. I call it Acclimation. The resistance starts going away, and it begins to feel like what you are doing is the natural thing to do.

Here's how this ties back to Awareness and Will Power. When we get some Awareness and Will Power, we can use them to start or develop a new habit (what I call a Routine). That way, twenty-one days later it'll have a life of its own, and you won't need more Awareness or Will Power to keep it going.

Then, the next time you get Awareness or Will Power, use them to start a NEW habit, and repeat the cycle. When you do, you'll become so productive you won't even believe it.

The goal is to work in a way that creates not only great results but also satisfaction and enjoyment for us. We don't need to become robots that just produce results, but we also don't need to get swept away by things that give us immediate pleasure but cost us results we'd proud of having, that make a difference in our life.

What Makes People Happy On The Job?

-- **Work for a company with fewer than one hundred people (25 percent more likely to be happy).**
-- **Supervise. (Managers and supervisors are 27 percent more likely to be happy.)**
-- **Work at something related to caregiving or direct service (75 percent more likely to be happy).**
-- **Have a skilled trade (50 percent more likely to be happy than the unskilled).**
-- **Be older. People in their 40s are the least happy.**

Happiness at Work survey, Nic Marks, nef (new economics foundation, London) 20twelve

Another important element that's often overlooked is that it's the TRANSITIONS that often trip us up. If you want to start going to the gym, you have to plan for the 'on ramp'. If you don't, and spend time looking for your clothes, shoes, or keys, your time gets cut short, causing you to fail before you even get started. The same goes for your 'off ramp' when you get done working out and re-join your track for the rest of your day.

Planning for these ramps will increase the chance that the new ritual will stick, and reduce your anxiety and sense of 'rushing'.

Most people who are trying to learn a new habit or ritual use Will Power to move through it. If you do so, you will probably find that after half an hour or an hour, you are exhausted. The moment you are exhausted, you will go back to your former habits because there is simply no more energy left. After a few days of this, you will conclude that you are incapable of learning a new habit.

I once saw a lady in my practice who wanted to learn three new habits at the same time. I explained to her that she was setting herself up to fail. Those entrepreneurs I work with who get this point go on to design very effective work schedules.

The quality aspect of focus is WHAT you are focusing on. For example, the outcome you want rather than just the work in front of you.

Additionally, as we build our ability to focus on just one thing at a time, we want to work on our ability to focus for longer and longer periods of time. That's the quantity aspect. Right now, how long can you work on one thing at a time before you go check your email or voicemail? And how many different things do you focus on during the day?

We want to work our way up to focus for a full forty-five minutes on just one thing. Most people don't focus on one thing long enough to get big results. We want to fix that.

In life, we have a few leverage points that can give us tremendous results. These are things we usually have to be proactive about, to go and get done. These include things such as educating ourselves, working out, etc. You must be the one to decide to do these things. If you have a business, there are just a few places where most of the leverage exists. The same goes for your relationships and health.

Most times when someone starts something and they cannot carry on or they procrastinate, it's either because they don't know how or they have unmet emotional needs. I have found that when you can break something down to fifteen-minute chunks, it becomes something that you can do.

The converse of the above is that if you cannot break down a project into doable fifteen-minute chunks, you cannot even start the project. I have written twenty books, published about ten of them, and developed new business projects using this rule. When I cannot provide chapter headings for the main ten or twelve chapters of the book in fifteen minutes, I know I am not ready to write the book.

When you don't know how to do something, you simply need to learn how to do it. For example, you are supposed to balance your check-book, but keep procrastinating. Finally, you can't put it off any longer, but when you sit down to do it you don't know what to do because your business manager who normally does it is now on vacation. Simply having someone walk you through the steps once or twice would have solved the problem.

Difficult goals do not raise motivation and learning when the skills needed to attain them are absent. You may need to learn how to set goals that are proximal, specific, and moderately difficult. In traditional education grading with a normal distribution curve, only a few students will do well, some will always fail, and the rest will lie in between. Goal-setting research in education has established the importance of proximal, specific, and moderately-challenging goals; they are beneficial for motivation and learning. You need to learn the process and you need to develop the habit, in a repeatable, ongoing fashion, of setting goals that are challenging and achievable.

The effect of group goal setting on group performance is similar to the effect of individual goal setting. When you see your goal, make sure you see yourself having obtained your goal. When you do not achieve your goal you can become disappointed with yourself for not achieving it.

By learning to accept feedback and constructive criticism, you will be able to expand your thinking and become much more creative. Part of setting good goals is thinking about how you will achieve them. The important part of the process is how you manage that change and how you can grow as a result.

You may choose to have an accountability partner. If you are doing the online coaching version of Freedom Formula, every time you have a coaching call you have the opportunity to be held accountable.

In order to get leverage if you just focused on three things, for forty-five minutes each, and did this every single day, what would those three things be? Make the list.

Next, what would the outcome be if you focused on each of these three things for the next three-five years. Write down the actions required for each of them.

It's important to focus on what you want to achieve, not on what you want to avoid. Your unconscious mind doesn't know how to get rid of the "Don't" part of a thought, so if you're focused on the negative you'll attract more of it into your life.

For example, if you say to yourself, "Don't drink, don't drink, don't drink", your unconscious minds hears "Drink... drink... drink."

You may want to find out what you are really good at. You may have some ideas yourself, but you can also get objective feedback from people around you. Sometimes you may have taken on someone else's idea of what you are good at. You may even have convinced yourself that you are good at something because your best friend or your father was good at that. So it's important to be objective.

What do you enjoy or what would you enjoy given a chance? It's important that you explore and discover what really excites you.

So focus on achieving positive outcomes, not avoiding negative ones. At the same time, it's important that you are honest with yourself about what you want more of in your life and what you want less of.

You may want to test different types of businesses or opportunities if you have not done so. Sometimes you may have some idealistic or romantic notions that may not stand the test of time. You may want to do a medical degree because you want to help others. You start on a medical course then discover that you cannot stand the idea of drawing blood.

Renewal

The concept of renewal may be the most important idea of all when it comes to becoming more productive and successful. Our bodies, emotions, and minds have natural systems where they renew themselves. They get rid of the junk, replace the sick cells, put new ones in place, etc. The interesting insight here is that these processes can't be impacted consciously.

You can't just say, "OK, stop feeling depressed right now", or

"OK, start attacking the cancer cells" to make it happen.

When you realize this, you'll understand the power of renewal and how to use it. You'll understand that you need to provide yourself with basic building blocks so your systems can renew themselves automatically, as they're designed to. You'll also need to stop doing the things that prevent these systems from renewing themselves.

On a physical level, most people want to feel better, more energetic, etc. If you don't feel this way, you're probably not giving your body the necessary building blocks. Water is one of these building blocks.

On an emotional level, we have processes that let us take advantage of opportunities and become optimistic, and processes that put us in a natural cycle of grieving when we lose something special to us. But many people block these natural emotional cycles, often with tension.

Inspire positive emotions by doing things that make you feel good inside, e.g. mentoring someone, doing something for another without expecting anything in return, etc.

On a mental level, the mind has processes to keep ourselves mentally healthy, for example with sleep and dreaming. If you don't know what to do to avoid blocking these processes, you won't be operating as well as you can.

One super important key here is to learn how to rest correctly and deeply, rather than resist resting or experience anxiety about resting. Pay attention to when you start feeling tired or unfocused. It's your body telling you there's a cycle that needs to be honored.

Your digestive system is super important. Chew your food thoroughly. Eat small meals and try not to snack between. Drink water about thirty minutes before a meal instead of drinking with the meal (it dilutes your stomach acid).

Your respiratory system is also, obviously, critical. Practice breathing from your stomach — like a baby does — instead of from your upper chest.

Your muscular and skeletal system is vital. Your body balances itself when it's moving. Spend thirty-sixty minutes a day moving your body. Stretch. Your immune system is important, too. Eat raw and organic foods when you can.

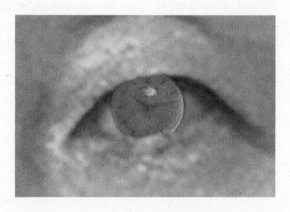

Time Cycles (*Seasons in a Man's Life*, Daniel Levinson)

There are certain natural time cycles that everyone goes through. We can choose to work with these time cycles or be out of synch with them. Most of us normally work with these cycles of time in an instinctive, automatic fashion.

The overview below is a summary from the very excellent book *The Seasons of a Man's Life* by Daniel Levinson. For the purposes of managing time, I will draw a very sharp distinction between the use of willpower and goal setting at different times in our lives.

There are many theories and models about developmental psychology and life structures. These include the likes of Urie Bronfenbrenner, Erik Erikson, Sigmund Freud, Jean Piaget, Barbara Rogoff, Esther Thelen, and Lev Vygotsky.

Life structure refers to the underlying pattern in an individual's life at any given point in time. A person's life structure is shaped mainly by his social and physical environment, and it primarily involves family and work.

There are six stages of adulthood in Levinson's book. From early childhood up to age twenty-two, the use of willpower in running one's life and in goal setting is crucial. In fact, those who fail to do so pay the price by not having these faculties developed later on in life. This is when the 10,000-hour rule comes into play.

However, after age twenty-two, willpower must be used more and more sparingly because it ends up exhausting your cognitive, affective, and conative aspects of your psyche. The cognitive part of the brain measures intelligence, the affective deals with emotions, and the conative drives how one acts on those thoughts and feelings.

Once these faculties are exhausted, you will go back to making choices the way you have always done. You become a legal adult at eighteen or twenty-one, depending on the laws of your country or state, but you reach your biological adulthood only at thirty-five. Once this occurs, the rate at which your cells break down speeds up. So the energy required to exert the use of your willpower will be used up faster.

So the more the number of positive habits you have to develop to manage your life better, the harder it gets. It's therefore crucial that you develop the right habits as early as you can. If you want to successfully manage time later (after thirty-five) in your life, learn the right habits first. Keeping to a regular schedule of waking up on time, having all your meals on time, sleeping on time, etc.... all these seemingly-small habits contribute.

In Levinson's Life Structure theory there are two key concepts:

1. The Stable Period — This is the time when a person makes crucial choices in life.
2. The Transitional Period — This is the end of one stage of adulthood and the beginning of a new one. Life during these transitions can be uncertain but the quality and significance of one's life commitments often change between the beginning and end of a period.

DO you have the following habits/routines/DMs in place?

- **Identifying the Core Priority**
- **Waking up**
- **Getting ready to work**
- **Winding down before sleep**
- **Dealing with relationships (Work and Personal)**
- **Dealing with Challenges**
- **Problem Solving**
- **Renewal (physical, emotional and mental)**

Compulsive Life	Designed Life
I rise to the occasion	I have key habits in place for my life
I am totally spontaneous at all times	I identify the key priority before I act
I am very fit and healthy	I have habits that keep me fit and healthy

C) IMPLEMENT

9) Execute Your Plan And Course Correct.

https://youtu.be/8w_rX3lIgLE

13

HOW DO YOU PUT IT ALL TOGETHER?

*Pick my left pocket of its silver dime, but spare
the right — it holds my golden time!*

Oliver Wendell Holmes

As you manage time and energy for a fulfilling life by planning for one hour daily, you will discover that it affects other areas of your life. Life Design for greater productivity is be a major life choice that shapes you in lots of ways.

Do you recall being asked the following questions?

- Do you want to do things faster?
- Do you want to achieve more with less effort?
- Do you want to have a higher quality of life?

All these specific questions concern the sort of life you may appreciate. If you'd answered "Yes" to all these questions, you were not just saying you had what it requires to manage your priorities for greater productivity and satisfaction; more importantly, you were validating the life that you wanted to lead.

No one is saying that Life Design for greater productivity will be painless, and no one ever will. Although Life Design for greater productivity will offer you tons of benefits along with skills to apply in life, remember that it will take some effort to get there. You have to be dedicated to embark on this program. Life Design for greater productivity can serve an essential role in your life just by helping you to cultivate positive qualities.

Always look at Life Design as a lifestyle instead of a goal; you then find it easier to adopt practices that augment your success. The adjustments in your schedule has a bigger purpose beyond realizing a single objective.

Be sure to analyze what is needed before embarking on a Life Design program. Planning in advance, scheduling events in fifteen-minute chunks, and building in buffer time should be regarded as essential prerequisites for Life Design for a superior life. Although our discussion is specific to Life Design for greater productivity, much of it will change apparently unrelated areas of your life.

There are many books on Time Management and/or Life Planning available. The model I'm presenting in this book is lean to the point of being minimalistic. But — and it's essential to keep this in mind — the reason for this is that you have to prepare intensively, both physically and mentally, with this model.

Stress and Work:

-- **76 percent put money and work as leading causes of stress in their lives.**
-- **41 percent are stressed out during the workday, an increase from 36 percent a year ago.**
-- **58 percent say they have the resources to manage stress.**
-- **Only 10 percent do their best thinking at work.**
-- **Workers are 45 percent less likely to come up with a new idea or solve a problem on days when under extreme pressure.**

Research by Top ten Online Colleges, 2013, USA

Planning in three- or five-year chunks is the key to major routines. If you fall off the wagon, pick yourself up and carry on. Eventually your habits will kick in and help you past the troubled spot. You will be better prepared for any stumbling block because you will be stronger. You will begin to think differently. You will be more positive about yourself overall. You will remember that you are a focused individual, that you need to make the necessary changes to reflect that.

Get into the practice of planning in three- or five-year chunks so you typically know what to do next. Take the time to learn necessary skills.

As essential as planning in three- or five-year chunks is planning for each task in fifteen-minute chunks. Anytime you observe people who effectively manage time for greater productivity, you will see that they plan for a task in fifteen-minute chunks. It is because they perceive the value of this practice.

Planning for a task in fifteen-minute chunks results in having achievable goals, and gives you peace of mind. Since you know in advance what to do in each minute of the fifteen-minute sequence, you will not procrastinate. You will know in advance if targets are achievable. The thrill of victory you continually experience by planning for each task in fifteen-minute chunks creates a positive feedback loop in your brain for greater success.

When implementing your Life Design program, there are several additional things to keep in mind. Encourage yourself by recalling the reasons you are doing this in the first place. Keep a favorable outlook; it'll serve you when discouraging moments come up. Break down long-term goals into specific tasks. You are more likely to remember exactly which guidelines and techniques worked for you before. Think about what you can do to enhance your routine, and move on from there.

Typical Mistakes Made When You Manage Time

Although slip-ups will happen any time you strive for a goal, whenever you take action, there are a couple of behaviors in particular you want to avoid at all costs.

Neither procrastinate nor vacillate. Both will negate your best efforts. Why would a person do all that work merely to reverse what he has done? This is what results when you procrastinate.

Provided you are consistent with your duties and see through the preparations, then you would be capable of good follow through.

Avoid energy vampires. It's useful to look at your life and find the things that rob you of energy. Your car has a motor. If it's tuned correctly, it'll run at the optimal level of efficiency. But if you have a couple of spark plugs unscrewed a little bit, some oil is missing, etc., then if it was supposed to be a 500-horsepower motor, maybe now you'll be lucky to get 200 out of it.

There may be things in our lives, outside our awareness, that are robbing us of energy. They are parasitic and they suck our energy subtly. They could be friends and relationships that drain you dry and leave you feeling exhausted and washed out. If you could invest in the $50 late fees on a credit card for twenty years, you'd be a millionaire. But you often don't recognize this.

As we've previously explored, effective Life Design requires quite a lot out of you. You need to be focused, relentless, and enlightened. Planning for a journey as impactful as great Life Design may actually help you get more 'real' about life.

You begin to see yourself as you are. These are some procedures you should incorporate that will help you nurture these qualities. Preparing your consciousness for the hard task of planning well for Life Design can be initially time-consuming, and you will most likely be putting in close to one hour daily initially to get ready. This will allow you ample time to ingrain these procedures into your routine.

Break long-term plans into short-term goals. This is helpful if you are planning in three- or five-year chunks. This will let you will know in advance if resources are available. This is not the only benefit that implementing this rule will bring: taking the time to learn the necessary skills and planning for the unexpected will be additional benefits.

You need to know what to do each minute of every fifteen-minute chunk. This is surely an ideal rule to reflect as you are planning for each task in fifteen-minute chunks. It will good to know in advance if targets are achievable. If you consider yourself as relentless, then it will be very simple for you to incorporate these procedures in your lifestyle.

Let us consider our instructions for planning backwards from five years to the present. It will require yet another degree of focus during the preparation period, but it'll be worth it. As you are working on having a clear, detailed to-do list, and having a clear sense of direction, you want to be able to break down long-term goals into specific tasks. Through doing this process regularly, you can have peace of mind.

It is these virtues that will guide you towards success when you finally manage time for greater productivity. So, remember to plan in three- or five-year chunks, plan backwards from five years to the present, and plan for each task in fifteen-minute chunks. Follow these specific tips and you will be unstoppable in no time!

What You Need to Know Before Starting a Life-Design Program

We discussed some of the various practices that a person who expects to manage time for greater productivity should think of doing. The probability, given that you have recognized the choices of an individual desiring to manage time for greater productivity, is that some choices are already woven into your everyday routine.

You should examine how you can incorporate these habits into a substantial part of your life. This will make priming to manage time for greater productivity a painless transition.

Nonetheless, preparing to realize major, long-term objectives will require you to make some adjustments in your routine. Your tolerance to personal growth pangs will be the determining factor in how rapidly you realize your ambitions.

Are you prepared to plan? Are you prepared to schedule events in fifteen-minute chunks and build in buffers? These were merely certain practices to equip you during the journey of Life Design for a fulfilling life. If it seems mind-boggling, don't fret. We have some tips to help you.

Don't Dart Through The Introductory Steps

Occasionally it seems like the introductory steps can be omitted. Perhaps you believe you can flourish without doing measures like planning in advance.

There will come a point after beginning Life Design for greater productivity when you experience a task like planning in three- or five-year chunks. If you did the planning well at the introductory stage, you will experience a considerably smoother time accomplishing your calling.

Do Not Call It Quits If You Mess Up Preparing

Regardless of how careful and well-directed your efforts may be, expect problems. Instead of pursuing perfection, take pleasure in small wins; they will add up to consistent gains. If you make a mistake, you are truly learning more about yourself and what works.

The key is to visualize how your future would change for the better once you became more organized and efficient. That should provide you enough motivation to start the journey to managing your time better.

Anytime the mind is geared toward the tasks ahead, it makes doing the work swifter. Everything we do begins with an idea. Plant positive ideas in your intellect, and the journey to manage time for greater productivity will really get underway.

Anytime You Think Of Giving Up, Don't

It is common to become discouraged as things become difficult. If Life Design for fulfilling life was painless, everyone would be doing it. The truth is that Life Design for great life initially takes a little energy and purposeful action. Then the momentum of your habits takes over, and the results can be very fulfilling.

With TV, the Internet, and social media so ubiquitous in our life, you may have preconceived opinions about Life Design. Life Design is really about finding out what matters to you.

Top managers have less stress than most. People with leadership positions show lower levels of cortisol and lower self-reported levels of anxiety. They have a larger sense of control that they use to fight stress. The more subordinates and power, the bigger the difference. *Ann Cuddy, Harvard Business School, Proceedings of the National Academy of Sciences, 2012*

Although Life Design for greater productivity begins with a journey within yourself, the material aspects are similarly critical. Even with your will in place, you ultimately have to work on physical preparations.

A practice takes a moment to bring into action. It begins with a commitment in the mind. Carry a journal to track the progression; it will encourage you to remain on track. If you go off track, get right back on!

Also, make sure you're enjoying your experience. Anybody who yearns to manage time for greater productivity also expects some intellectual gratification from it. Feed off the recognition you get along the way as you eventually manage a day at work successfully!

Set Priorities and Establish Goals

What are the truly important things in life for you? How would you rank them?

With your priorities established, you can now set goals that match them. Goals are most effective when they are organized on a daily, weekly, monthly, and annual basis. For example, if a priority is to remain physically healthy, a goal can be to lose a certain number of pounds within one year, with shorter-term goals of exercising four times per week for thirty minutes.

You may want to make a goal board, with a bunch of pictures that represent the outcomes you want.

Review the outcome you're looking for before you sit down and focus on each specific area. Write down a few compelling outcomes you'd like to achieve physically, emotionally, and mentally, how achieving each would make you feel, what deeper benefits each would provide to your life.

It's also important that you are clear about why you want to achieve a particular goal. If you do not have a strong reason or you're dutifully fulfilling your parents' dreams, you are likely to be very disappointed or unfulfilled at the end.

Criteria for Achieving Outcomes:

- **Definition** — Be as specific as possible in defining your objective. Include all the elements that might be involved. Define the outcome in visual, auditory, and kinesthetic terms.
- **Agency** — It must depend on you and you only.
- **Purpose** — Why do you want to achieve this goal? What will it do for you?
- **Need to Know** — What do you need to know to accomplish this goal? Try to anticipate all the information you need.

- **Resource** — What strengths do you have that will enable you to accomplish the goal? How can you best utilize them?
- **Roadblocks** — What may prevent you from accomplishing the goal?
- **Steps** — How will you accomplish your goal? List each possible step and include the date that you accomplish it.
- **Miscellaneous** — What else can you think of that is important with respect to this goal?

Outcomes can be set in any of these eight areas:

a. Healthy-Eating Habits
b. Exercise
c. Stress Management
d. Fine-Tuning My Emotional Intelligence
e. Creating and Managing Priorities
f. Time Management
g. Developing a New Business
h. Developing New Skills

Example of Setting Specific Goals in Major Areas

For an example of listing two goals in all eight areas:

A. Healthy-Eating Habits

1. To eat a healthy breakfast daily
2. To lose three kg steadily in three months

B. Exercise

1. To do forty-five-minute walks three times a week
2. To be able to do at least thirty sit-ups three times a week

C. Stress Management

1. To stop drinking coffee and drink herbal teas instead
2. To have a relaxed body posture daily

D. Fine-Tuning My Emotional Intelligence

1. To spend fifteen minutes a day talking to my mate
2. To listen to my co-workers and find out what matters to them

E. Creating and Managing Priorities

1. To work out my top three priorities for work at the beginning of the day
2. To decline non-essential projects

F. Time Management

1. To get home by 7 pm daily
2. To finish all my work in the office so weekends are free

G. Developing Daily Peak Performance Triggers

1. To get myself all ready for going to work
2. To learn techniques so that I am calm and relaxed in a crisis

H. Developing New Skills

1. To learn the new computer spreadsheet program
2. To take up sailing

Criteria List For Achieving Outcomes (Worked Example)

Let's look at an example: "Learn the new computer spreadsheet program."

A   Definition: "Learn and be able to apply the computer spreadsheet program at work in three weeks. I will be able to use the program and complete my work 50 percent faster."

B   Purpose: "I want to learn the program to improve my work efficiency so that I no longer need to take work home."

C   Need to Know: "I need to find out where I can do such a program."

D   Resource: "I have learned other computer programs easily."

E   Roadblocks: "I am afraid of making a fool of myself in class. So I may delay signing up for the program. I also have visitors next week, so I need to delay taking up classes."

F   Steps: "I have already found a suitable computer-training school. The course will take about two weeks, two hours a day, three times a week. I will start after next week, so in three weeks I will be able to use the program."

G   What else can you think of that is important with respect to this goal?: "Nothing Else."

Start on your program. If something unexpected comes up, take a rain check and carry on when ready.

The real issue is not whether you have enough time; the issue is whether you are using your time well. Do you know what your true priorities are? If you don't know, you've got a problem. If you know what your true priorities are, are you living in a way that honors those priorities every day? If not, again, you've got a problem.

Clarifying your priorities sometimes requires being brutally honest with yourself and making some tough choices. It also might take some soul searching as well as serious research and study in order to master the best strategies for achieving whatever your particular goal happens to be.

Success sometimes requires that you redesign your life so that you can honor your priorities. Success usually necessitates structures to remind yourself of your priorities in an ongoing, day-to-day way. But first you must clarify what your priorities are.

Exercise 1 — My Priorities

Make a short list of your top five-ten priorities. You are unique, your priorities will be unique, and so be incredibly honest with yourself about what truly matters to you.

Exercise 2 — Priority Objectives

Now, looking over your list of priorities, create a current primary objective for that area of your life or business. It may be a short-term measurable goal, such as "Increase my current client base to X by <date>", or it may be an ongoing objective such as exercise for at least thirty minutes three times per week.

I am a big fan of weekly planning. I recommend that you schedule a regular day and time each week to take at least fifteen minutes to set some objectives for the week and to schedule when you will focus on certain projects. When you do your weekly planning, be sure to have your short list of priorities and objectives handy.

Look over the list and make sure you're actually prioritizing those things that are most important in your planning and actions. One of my favorite exercises to do with my coaching clients is a 'Priorities Wheel'. This simple process is always energizing and clarifying. It provides a guiding light and a road map to success.

Exercise 3 — Priorities Wheel

1. Choose a goal or vision you would like to achieve. Write your goal or a statement summarizing your vision at the top of the Priorities Wheel on the following page.
2. Label the Wheel with eight priorities to focus on in order to achieve your vision or goal.

3. Score your sense of satisfaction with each of your priorities on a scale from 0 to 10. For each priority ask yourself, "On a scale of 0-10, how well am I focusing on and implementing this priority?"

4. What would a score of ten look like for each of your priorities? What actions would you be taking, what results will you be getting, and how would that feel? How will you know when it is a 10?

5. Decide what actions you are willing to take in order to move your satisfaction with each of your priorities towards a 10. Write them down. Put them on your to-do list or in your calendar.

- Increase Productive Activities: Learn to distinguish between activity (busy work) [A], accomplishments (actions taken to accomplish goals) [B], and productivity (actions taken to become more productive and efficient, i.e. to do more in less time with less resources) [C]. Make a 'To-Do List' then categorize your activities under A, B, or C. Once you've identified all your [A] activities, eliminate them. Focus all your energy first on the [B] activities and then on the [C] activities.

- Decrease Time Wasters: Don't expect yourself to do everything. Learn to politely and firmly say "No" at times, based on your priorities and goals. Delegate tasks when possible. Handle each piece of paper, mail, or email only once, i.e., either respond to it or dispose of it. Keep routinely used items in the same place so they can be located immediately when needed. Group similar mundane tasks (reading/responding to mail, making phone calls, etc.,) and schedule specific times to do them on a daily/weekly basis.

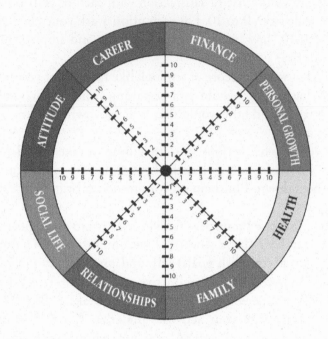

PRIORITIES WHEEL

Compulsive Life	**Designed Life**
I rise to the occasion	I have key priorities around which I design my life
I have problems saying "No"	I say "Yes" only to core priorities

To have more impact in your life, join Dr Sundardas for a deep dive Master Class called **"How To Earn Six Figures in Six Months"**, our gift to you. Visit **http://mylife-bydesign.com/masterclass**

https://youtu.be/3uPK_GGInUk

14

AN OVERVIEW OF YOUR LIFE DESIGN PROGRAM

"The secret of getting ahead is getting started. The secret of getting started is breaking your complex overwhelming tasks into small manageable tasks, and then starting on the first one."

Mark Twain

If you are committed to great Life Design you will put in systems that work. If you are not, you are likely to struggle and continue to make excuses for your failure.

Life Design for a fulfilling life not only physically challenges you but also stimulates your mind. Regarding planning the overall strategy, multi-faceted footwork is surely essential. There may be tons of tools available, but your personal discernment will be a better option than any tool. After all, you perceive your own body and state of mind like no one else. Apply that information to calculate your mark and don't doubt your intuition as it's not likely to misguide you.

We calculated that the typical duration an individual needs to manage time for greater productivity is one hour daily. So you need to be generous while planning your time. If you require more time or less time, adjust accordingly. Lastly, adjust your objectives accordingly.

As you get ready to manage time for greater productivity, you may come across other people looking to accomplish the same objective, albeit with a different timeframe. Don't get caught up wrestling with their schedule or techniques if it does not work with your everyday rhythm. This is why some people get tired and finally surrender.

You've taken the first big step; now carry on at your own pace. Compulsive people rush into things based on sudden enthusiasms. Instead, start out slow and, as your preparations progress and you become clearer and more confident about what works, gradually put in more energy working on your goal.

63 percent of financial advisers who described themselves as lacking time management skills and discipline experienced health issues, including sleep apnea and high blood pressure.
Health of Advisors Report, 9/2008

Although the methods described here aren't foolproof, they are the ideal starting points for newbies looking to manage time for greater productivity. There are many, many tips you can use for your preparation stage, since you know your state of mind.

Apply this information, along with the plan revealed here. to get out there and finally manage time for greater productivity! If you are consistent with how you schedule your time, and apply the information here to calculate a workable strategy, you will be a great success in no time!

Dos and Don'ts of Life Design

The notion of Life Design for greater productivity can be exciting as well as scary. The distinguished Peter Drucker, who is acknowledged as the father of Modern Management, wrote, *"One cannot buy, rent or hire more time. The supply of time is totally inelastic. No matter how high the demand, the supply will not go up."*

> ## OVERVIEW OF THE PLANNING AND IMPLEMENTATION PROCESS
>
> **Do Planning in Advance**
>
> **Don't Procrastinate**
>
> **Do Schedule Events In fifteen-Minute Chunks**
>
> **Don't Vacillate**
>
> **Do Plan in Three- Or Five-Year Chunks**
>
> **Don't Interrupt the Process**
>
> **Do Plan for Each Task In fifteen-Minute Chunks**
>
> **Don't Distract Yourself**

> ## OVERVIEW OF WRAPPING UP THE PROJECT PROCESS
>
> **Do Wrap Up the Project**
>
> **Don't Drag Closing Down the Project**
>
> **Do Prepare for The Next Item on The To-Do List**
>
> **Don't Delay Moving on to the Next Piece**

The following are ten tips to manage your priorities:

1. **Do not confuse 'busyness' with productivity.** Highly productive people are often less busy than those who are overworked and overwhelmed.

2. **Do not confuse the urgent with the important.** Last-minute distractions from yourself and others are not necessarily priorities.

3. **The key to time management** is **self-management**.

4. **Remember the 80/20 Rule of time management**, which tells us that 80 percent of the importance of what we do in any given day lies in only 20 percent of the activities. Therefore, if you focus on accomplishing the top 20 percent of the most important tasks, you will feel more productive and satisfied at the end of the day.

5. **Use a good day planner.** The best ones give you at least one full page (or screen) per day, with space allocated for each working hour of the day.

6. **Separate obligatory time from discretionary time.** In your day planner, block out all the times when you're committed to others to be at a certain place at a certain time, such as meetings, conferences, and other appointments. What's not your obligatory time is your discretionary time. This is the time you can manage.

7. **List:** At the beginning of each day, write down a bullet-point list of everything you would like to accomplish that day.

8. **Prioritize:** Next to each bullet-point item, assign an 'A' if this is a "must-do" item for today, a 'B' for "should-do" and a 'C' for "could-do". For large projects, break it down into small parts and prioritize. Divide-and-conquer.

9. **Implement:** Focus on accomplishing your 'A' list with your discretionary time. Check off each item as you complete it. With this system, even if you accomplish only 20 percent of the tasks in your list for the day, you still would have accomplished 80 percent of the most important work.

10. **What you don't finish today, transfer** to your list for tomorrow and reprioritize.

Key Points for LIFE DESIGN

Prioritizing, planning and scheduling is the process by which you design your life. By doing so you can reduce your stress levels and maximize your effectiveness.

Follow this nine-step process to prepare and implement:

1. Decide on the essential priorities necessary for you to succeed in your job/business/life.
2. Identify the time/resources you have available.
3. Identify what goals and targets you need to achieve.
4. Identify what is irrelevant, intrusive, and drains energy.
5. Eliminate habits and behaviors and commitments that do not serve you.
6. Create firewalls to protect your boundaries and learn to reject what doesn't serve you.
7. Schedule the goals and targets you need to achieve to meet your priorities.
8. Ensure that you have the right habits in place to achieve your targets.
9. Execute your plan and course correct.

It's crucial for your professional and personal goals that you schedule your time. If you have little or no discretionary time left when you reach Step 7 above, revisit your tasks to see if you can do them differently. Otherwise, your work-life balance will suffer.

Creating your Strategic Plan
(For the CEO, Entrepreneur, Manager)

This is a summary of all the exercises mentioned in the book:

1. *Identify the core business beliefs you need to succeed:* I believe the following things are true and they are how I want to run my business (Write down ten)
2. *Your Personal Vision*: Write out all that you want to be, have and do if money were no object. How much money would you like to have flow through your life to make this happen?
3. *Your Company Vision:* Write out your company vision as if it were already true (present tense). Include the value of your company and any other details you want to make sure happen for you.

4. *Your Ideal Future:* Write your ideal future here. Have fun with it!

5. *Long-Term Targets:* Pick a specific date somewhere between three and five years from now. Write down the long-term targets you want to have accomplished by that date for your business.

6. *Long-Term Priorities:* Write down the most important areas of your business to focus on in order to accomplish your long-term targets. Write down ten, but identify your top five and then write them down.

7. *Short-term Goals:* Pick a specific date somewhere about one year from now. Write down the short- term goal that you want to have accomplished by that date for your business.

8. *Top Five Short-term Areas of Focus:* Write down the most important areas of your business to focus on in order to accomplish your short-term goals. Write down ten then identify your top five.

9. *Key Metrics:* Write down all the things you may want to measure in your business. Write down the four things you will measure on a weekly basis to ensure you hit your short-term goals.

10. *Key Short-Term Area of Focus:* Detail what all the Weekly Tasks aim to accomplish.

11. *Quarterly Initiatives:* Write down your first Key Short-Term Area of Focus then break it down into no more than five quarterly initiatives.

12. *Weekly Tasks:* Break down each quarterly initiative for the upcoming quarter into smaller tasks. Write down how long each task will take. Go back and break down any tasks that are longer than thirty minutes into smaller tasks. You are done when all tasks on your list are no more than thirty minutes long.

Life Design For The CEO

Here are twelve time-management habits. Tailor these as you like, but whichever you're working on, ensure you do so in twenty-one-day cycles.

Habit 1: Strive to be authentic. Be as honest with yourself as you can about what you want and why you do what you do.

Habit 2: Favor trusting relationships. Build relationships with people you can trust and count on. Ensure those same people can trust and count on you. Train your staff to assume greater responsibility. This will free up your time.

Habit 3: Maintain a lifestyle that will give you maximum energy. This includes exercise for at least 120 minutes a week, sufficient sleep, and an appropriate lunch.

Habit 4: Listen to your biorhythms and organize your day accordingly. Schedule your tasks based on how your energy fluctuates throughout the day. Stop working impossible hours trying to do it all on your own.

Habit 5: Set very few priorities and stick to them. Plan your time so you are working on a maximum of two things, both of which are your highest priorities. The negative effects of bad meetings are much more dramatic than the positive impact of good sessions.

Habit 6: Turn down things that are inconsistent with your priorities. Saying "No" to other people will make you more productive.

Habit 7: Set aside time for focused effort. Schedule time every day to work on just one thing. We have spoken about how "attention fragmentation" afflicting the always-connected executive harms productivity and happiness.

Habit 8: Automate repetitive tasks and improve them if possible. Consider ways of doing things better and faster.

Habit 9: Build solid processes. Set up processes that last and run without your attention.

Habit 10: Spot trouble ahead and solve problems immediately. Anticipate potential problems and build solutions for them in advance.

Habit 11: Chunk up your work into small units. Focus on one unit at a time. Instead of dreaming about the big goal, spend most of your time working on what's in front of you.

Habit twelve: Unless there's a good reason to give it up, don't terminate what you considered worth starting. Stop doing what's no longer worthwhile; finish what's important.

Life Design For The Salesperson

Most sales people spend only ten percent of their available time selling!

- Active selling — 10 percent
- Prospecting — 10 percent
- Problem Solving — 14 percent
- Personal phone calls and e-mails — 17 percent
- Travel time — 18 percent
- Administration — 31 percent

Best Practices for Sales By the Numbers

- 10, 2 & 4 — time of day you check voicemail & e-mail
- 45 seconds — time it takes for customer to form an opinion of you
- 4 hours — longest length of time to return a customer's inbound call
- 2 — number of hours spent in creative thinking per week
- 3-4 hours/day — time spent in front of a customer
- 4-6 — number of face-to-face sales calls per week
- 4-8 — number of outbound proactive prospecting calls/day
- 5 — number of new large key accounts in development

Key to Successful Time Management for the Salesperson

- Spend more time with high-potential customers
- Spend more time with qualified leads and referrals
- Spend more time identifying customer needs and creating solutions
- Spend less time on administrative duties
- Spend less time on non-revenue-producing activities

Plan and Prioritize Your Day

- A — Most important, with serious consequences
- B — Something with only mild consequences
- C — Nice to do, with no consequences
- D — Delegate
- E — Eliminate

Work on the most important thing first!

- List A1, A2, A3, B1, B2, B3, C1, C2, C3
- Work on tasks that give key results:

  - Prospecting
  - Building rapport and trust
  - Identifying needs
  - Asking probing questions
  - Presenting the proposal persuasively
  - Answering objections
  - Closing the sale
  - Getting re-sales and referrals
  - Setting a Sales Goal fifty weeks/year and forty hours/day

Life Design For The Online Entrepreneur

Life Design for the online entrepreneur includes both Life Design for the CEO (above) and Life Design for the Salesperson (above). The rest of the day should have rituals focused on all the necessary follow-ups that are part and parcel of any business.

Successful people have a number of habits:

1. They Create Back-Up Plans.

Back-up plans can help you sleep easier at night. Back–up plans also mean you have considered the territory and know what is required. If somehow the worst does happen (and the "worst" is never as bad as you think) the backup plans mean that you have a variety of options that will help you find a way to rebound. As long as you keep working hard and keep learning from your mistakes, you always will.

2. They Do The Work.

You can be good with a little effort. You can be excellent with a little more effort.

But you can't be great--at anything- unless you put in an incredible amount of focused effort. Scratch the surface of any person with rare skills and you'll find a person who has put thousands of hours of effort into developing those skills.

There are no shortcuts. There are no overnight successes. Everyone has heard about the 10,000-Hour Principle but no one follows it… except remarkably successful people.

So start doing the work now. Time is a-wasting.

3. ...And They Work A *Lot* More.

Every extremely successful entrepreneur I know (personally) works more hours than the average person — *a lot more*. They have long lists of things they want to get done, so they have to put in lots of time. Better yet, they *want* to put in lots of time.

If you don't embrace a workload others would consider crazy then your goal doesn't mean that much to you, or it's not particularly difficult to achieve. Either way you won't be remarkably successful. Once you know how to do it, you then pass it on or outsource it.

4. They Avoid The Crowds.

Conventional wisdom yields conventional results. Joining the crowd — no matter how trendy the crowd or how 'hot' the opportunity — is a recipe for mediocrity. Remarkably successful people habitually do what other people won't do. They go where others won't go because there's a lot less competition and much greater chance for success.

5. They Start At The End...

Average success is often based on setting average goals. Decide what you really want: to be the best, the fastest, the cheapest, the biggest, whatever. Aim for the ultimate. Decide where you want to end up. *That* is your goal.

Then you can work backwards and lay out every step along the way. Never start small where goals are concerned. You'll make better decisions — and find it much easier to work a lot harder — when your ultimate goal is ultimate success.

6. . . . But They Don't Stop There.

Achieving a goal — no matter how huge — isn't the finish line for highly successful people. Achieving one huge goal just creates a launching pad for achieving another huge goal.

Maybe you want to create a $one hundred-million business; once you do that you can leverage your contacts and influence to create a charitable foundation for a cause you believe in. Then your business and humanitarian success can create a platform for speaking, writing, and thought leadership. The process of becoming remarkably successful in one field will give you the skills and network to be remarkably successful in many other fields. Remarkably successful people don't try to win just one race; they expect and plan to win a number of subsequent races.

7. They Sell.

I once asked several business owners and CEOs to name the one skill they felt contributed the most to their success. Each said the ability to sell.

Keep in mind selling isn't manipulating, pressuring, or cajoling. Selling is explaining the logic and benefits of a decision or position. Selling is convincing other people to work with you. Selling is overcoming objections and roadblocks.

Selling is the foundation of business and personal success. It is knowing how to negotiate, to deal with "No", to maintain confidence and self-esteem in the face of rejection, to communicate effectively with a wide range of people, to build long-term relationships.

When you truly believe in your idea, or your company, or yourself then you don't need to have a huge ego or a huge personality. You don't need to 'sell'. You need to just communicate.

8. They Are Never Too Proud.

To admit they made a mistake. To say they are sorry. To have big dreams. To admit they owe their success to others. To poke fun at themselves. To ask for help.

My Outcomes In Life (2017)

- **Current Situation**
- **Personal**
- **Business**
- **Community Work**

CURRENT SITUATION

I do not exercise regularly. I am probably not spending sufficient time out with my wife. I am working a little too hard. I often find myself working long hours to fire fight some situations. While parts of my business are extremely well-defined and have systems in place, others are less organized. Our seminar programs are often run on an ad-hoc basis. We need to systemize lead generation and conversion. While I know I need to be involved in more partnerships and grow a list of affiliates, I haven't been systematic about this.

Recently I put more emphasis on marketing and public relations in a focused fashion and put a team in place to handle this. We are still testing this team and growing it. We are in the process of launching different projects. This year, we have become more systematic about this.

In my five-year future model, the aim is to build systems for all of the above. I also want to prepare one of the companies for a pre-IPO process. The target is to achieve all this strategically without working longer hours.

PERSONAL

Health
Work at losing weight to get to eighty kg.
Daily walks with wife.
Start Tai Chi in 2017.

Relationships
Have two one-week holidays with wife (middle of the year and the end).
Every three months take a four-day break with wife.
Keep track of family events and anniversary.
Arrange a schedule of lunch and dinner appointments to keep up with friends and class reunions.

Personal Development
Ongoing training in profiling.
Ongoing training in professional development.

BUSINESS

Ensure I focus only on what requires my unique skill sets and increases my return on investment.

Marketing and PR
Develop a marketing and PR department to handle online and offline projects.

Partners
Setting up screening processes and structures for partners and JV partners.

Clinic
Automate and delegate processes that can be passed on.
Rebrand some niches.
Ten percent growth yearly for Clinic.

Seminar Company
Automate and delegate processes that can be passed on.
Develop JV relationships.
Rebrand some niches.
Ensure that we can go online effectively.
Target fifty percent growth years for next three years.

Wellness License Program
Develop partners in other countries.
Train coaches and facilitators.
Target is to be in six countries in the next three years, ten units a year.
To reach financial freedom in the next seven years.

COMMUNITY WORK

Facilitate the work of a charity that focuses on healthy and happy families.

You can assess well you are meeting your goals and targets by developing your own monitoring system for your exercise, nutrition, rest, and work schedules. Enclosed below is a sample chart. This is an example from how I track my state of focus and efficiency.

The code below indicates my grading system:

* Grade D, Barely following the program
** Grade C, Just about on target
*** Grade B, Doing well to meet targets
**** Grade A, Doing extremely well on the program

From doing the chart, I found out that when I slept badly (look at Tuesday), my emotions, how well I managed my states, my concentration, and my focus all suffered.

DAILY CHART FOR MONITORING SYSTEM AND STATE

	Mon	Tues	Wed	Thurs	Fri	Sat	Sun
Exercise	45m		45m		45m		
Diet	****	***	***	****	***	****	***
Number of meals	3	3	3	3	3	3	2
Snacks	2	3	2	3	3	3	4
Quantity of rest & recreation	45m	30m	15m	30m	45m	45m	120m
Time to bed	11pm	12 midnight	11pm	11pm	12 midnight	2am	11pm
Time to get up	6am	5am	6am	6am	6am	11am	6am
Hours of sleep	7hrs	5hrs	5hrs	6hrs	7hrs	9hrs	7hrs
Quality of sleep	****	**	***	****	****	***	****
Positive Attitude	****	**	***	***	****	***	****
Up Time State	****	**	***	***	****	****	****
Concentration	****	**	**	***	***	****	****
Warrior State	****	**	***	***	***	****	****
Peak State Strategies	***	*	**	***	***	****	****
Fun Today	***	*	**	**	***	****	****
Energy Level	***	*	**	**	***	***	****

Sample of Strategic Plan for one of my Companies. Notice there is only one priority: Lead-Generation Automation.

Integrated Strategic Plan Workbook Mind Strategics Learning Consultancy 2017										
Values	Abundance	Colloborate	Multiply Value	Strategic Innovation	Kaisen	Be Real	Embodied	Results Driven	Never give in, Never give up	Whatever you conceive, you achieve
Vision	Thriving business growth consultancy and products company. We have affiliates, strategic partners and partners with co-brands. We are sought after experts on business innovation. We drive $3 million in revenue with 60% net profit margin.									
My Big Dream	Take 2, 2 week vacations a year with no email, Own our own office space									
Long Term Targets	12/31/2020		Revenue $ 2,000,000		Net Profit $ 1,200,000		Full Time Systems		2, 2 week vacations a year, offline	
Long Term Areas of Focus	Marketing		Technology		Strategic Alliances		Product Development		Staffing	
Short Term Goals	12/31/2017		Revenue $ 300,000		Net Profit $ 180,000		Admin Support		Deposit for office	
Short Term Areas of Focus	Affiliate Teams		Automated Systems		Strategic Partnerships		Staffing		Buy New office	
Key Metrics	Revenue		Net Profit		# Proposals per week		Funnel Conversion		Total Debt	
Annual Theme	LEAD GENERATION AUTOMATION									

https://youtu.be/M3UnG2YJD-s

15

TOWARDS THE
EMERGING NEW YOU

*Time equals life; therefore, waste your time and waste
your life, or master your time and master your life.*

Alan Lakein

Life Design for greater productivity isn't for the faint hearted. It may be initially challenging, then, as new habits take over, it becomes effortless and rewarding.

To start with, you recognize how to manage time and energy for greater productivity. Whether you flourish or fail, understanding how to prepare will be valuable to know. There's a wealth of encouragement and knowledge that you may discover online or in self-help books, but there's nothing like beginning a program to manage your time for greater productivity to provide unique insights into how the various strategies work. And this sort of knowledge not only results in understanding yourself better but also and more importantly gives you much needed information for other endeavors.

Great Life Design for a fulfilling life should be an aspiration that many have, but only a few have the focus and preparation to complete it. Life Design for greater productivity proves your commitment in the eyes of other people; more importantly, it proves your commitment to yourself.

The guts along with the willpower it takes to perform Life Design for a fulfilling life remains a part of your personal treasure chest.

Life Design — The New Lifestyle

Individuals who strive to manage time for greater productivity come in all shapes and sizes. However, no matter the skill level, there are certain things in common among those who do time management and thrive on it. Very often they do well because they share certain lifestyle traits along with aligned habits. One of these traits must, obviously, include planning. Without it, Life Design for greater productivity and fulfilment would be next to impossible.

People with well-designed lives are typically good at knowing what to do next. They also take the time to learn the necessary skills. These are not mystical powers that you somehow gain when you elect to manage time for greater productivity; they are traits you gradually incorporate into your life the more deeply you get into managing your time for a fulfilling life.

As you train for a great Life Design, you will discover that these lifestyle adjustments are taking place in your routine. Planning in three- or five-year chunks along with planning for each task in fifteen-minute chunks makes sense in a lot of ways. As a result, you understand what you need to do next along to have achievable goals. The lifestyle is challenging — and unquestionably worth it.

Common Questions

By now, you may be mindful of the steps you need to take to manage time for greater productivity. Say you think of an issue that hasn't been handled yet. Do not fret. Following are some common points that surface with Life Design for a fulfilling life:

- Be very clear about what your priorities are.
- A major tip is to value your time.
- Be realistic about time and processes.

A different question that typically comes up as people are planning to manage time for greater productivity is what 'rules' are necessary for Life Design for a fulfilling life. These are certain guidelines to keep in mind:

- While planning in three- or five-year chunks, break long-term plans into short-term goals. This will let you know in advance if resources are available.
- Typically, it is essential to plan for each task in fifteen-minute chunks. This will let you know in advance if targets are achievable.
- As you zoom in on planning backwards from five years to the present, be sure you are able to break down long-term goals into specific tasks. This will grant you peace of mind.

You have successfully taken the initial step toward Life Design for a fulfilling life by reading this book. More questions will undoubtedly surface; another way you may help yourself is by tackling this initiative with a companion with similar objectives.

Many times, the 'buddy system' is a great solution when tackling an aspiration that requires a focused and relentless nature. Although you can, ultimately, manage by yourself your time for greater productivity, it makes sense to pair up with someone upon the same journey to discuss challenges as they arise. Be conscious to choose like-minded companions; avoid people who may be unmotivated or slow, as they will guide you away from tackling your goals.

Remember the questions you answered a little while ago?

Do you want to do things faster?
Do you want to achieve more with less effort?
Do you want to have a higher quality of life?

You have answered "Yes" to these questions; this determined you had the correct spirit to succeed at Life Design. Choose a companion who will also unequivocally answer "Yes" to these questions as they also are likely to be more inclined to succeed at great Life Design. Work in tandem with this companion.

Personal Upgrades

This program is about becoming an upgraded version of you, a version beyond any vision for yourself that you can see right now. One of our most amazing abilities is to imagine an upgraded version of ourself — and then go to work to make it happen.

Most of us have fallen prey to processes that hold us back. One of these fatal flaws is tending to "Paint our past into our future", i.e. painting our future based on our past, rather than painting something totally new and without limits. Another thing to realize is that when we resist something in our lives, we are really giving it energy. As Carl Jung said, "Whatever you resist, persists."

Notice the things you're resisting in life, and let them go. Stop giving energy to them. Another powerful technique is to 'manufacture optimism'. One thing that distinguishes high-level athletes and other high performers from the rest of us is their ability to create optimism, no matter what situation they're in.

Emotional states, like optimism, come from internal comparison. If you want to make yourself feel bad, compare yourself to other people who have more than you, or remember how good you used to have it then think of how bad you have it now.

To feel better, start comparing yourself to others who have less than you, or think of how good you have it right now then focus on your progress instead of how much further you still have to go.

Next, finding a mentor is one of the most powerful things you can do to feed your own transformation. A mentor can see the next level of 'you', a 'you' that you yourself can't see yet. They've seen other people grow from your level to the next, so they can see that future for you, and tell you exactly how to get there in as few steps as possible.

Always try to have at least one mentor in your life at all times. It can literally transform your life. At different times in my life I have had mentors and coaches for different parts of my life and or business. A mentor or coach offers you the fastest possible route to the upgraded you.

Conclusion

Life Design for greater productivity is no easy task, and sometimes you may not invest enough time in recovery after managing a day at work successfully. So much effort is invested on preparing, yet hardly any thought is contributed to the recovery strategy. Although focusing on Life Design for a fulfilling life is essential, you may also want to consider what all you would like to achieve after you've achieved all your goals. There is no doubt you will feel more positive about yourself after achieving your aspirations.

Best wishes on Life Design for a greater, more productive future!

For personal development programs for a New You, click on:

www.yourmindstrategy.com/LIVE/events/success-permission

BIBLIOGRAPHY

1. Kochanek, K. D., Murphy, S. L., Xu, J., & Tejada-Vera, B. "Deaths: Final Data for 2014." National Vital Statistics Reports, 2017
2. Schwartz, T. "The Power of Full Engagement." National Safety Council, Priority Magazine, 1-2/2007
3. Research by Top Ten Online Colleges, USA. [Online]. Available: http://www.top10onlinecolleges.org/cost-job-stress/, 2013
4. Sherman, G. D., Lee, J. J., Cuddy, A. J. C., Renshon, J., Oveis, C., Gross, J. J., Lerner, J. S. "Leadership is Associated with Lower Levels of Stress." *Harvard Business School, Proceedings of the National Academy of Sciences, 2012*
5. *"Sleep in America."* National Sleep Foundation, March 2008
6. Heinen, L., Darling, H. "Addressing Obesity in the Workplace: The Role of Employers." *Conference Paper,* The Obesity Society, *Centers for Disease Control and Prevention & RTI* International, 2009
7. Coulson, J. C., McKenna, J., Field, M. "Exercising at Work and Self-Reported Work Performance." *University of Bristol, Department of Exercise, Nutrition & Health Sciences, published in the International Journal of Workplace Health Management, 2008, Vol. 1, Issue 3*
8. Mandel M., Hamm S., Matlack S., Farrell C., Palmer C., Therese A. "The Real Reasons You're Working So Hard." Business Week, 00077135, 10/3/2005, Issue 3953 (p60)
9. *Caravan Opinion Research* Corp. Int'1/L.A. Times, *2000*
10. *Levinson,* D. The *Seasons of a Man's Life. Ballantine* Books, *1986.* ISBN: 978-0345339010
11. Marks, N. *"Happiness at Work." Survey.* London: *nef (new economics foundation), 2012*
12. Vessenes, K. "Advisers Can Work Less, Be Healthy and Make More Money." *Health of Advisors* Press *Report, 9/2008*

13. Rackham, N., *SPIN Selling.* New York: McGraw-Hill, 1988. ISBN: 0-07-051113-6
14. Satir, V., Banmen, J., Gerber, J., Gomori, M. *"The Satir Model."* Palo Alto, CA: Science and Behavior Books, 1991. ISBN: 0-8314-0078-1